EZRA POUND
The Legacy of Kulchur

EZRA

The

Edited by
Marcel Smith
and
William A. Ulmer

POUND

Legacy of Kulchur

The University of Alabama Press
Tuscaloosa and London

Copyright © 1988 by
The University of Alabama Press
Tuscaloosa, Alabama 35487
Manufactured in the United States of America

Library of Congress Cataloging-in-Publication Data

Ezra Pound

   Papers from the 12th Annual Alabama Symposium on English and American
Literature, October 24–26, 1985.
   "A selective bibliography on Pound's economic ideas": p.
   Bibliography: p.
   Includes index.
   1. Pound, Ezra, 1885–1972—Criticism and interpretation—
Congresses.   I.   Smith, Marcel.   II.   Ulmer, William A.   III.   Alabama
Symposium on Engish and American Literature (12th : 1985 : University of
Alabama)
PS3531.082Z6218   1988   811'.52   86-24999
ISBN 0-8173-0356-1
ISBN 0-8173-0383-9 (pbk.)
British Library Cataloguing-in-Publication Data is available.

Contents

Illustrations

EZRA POUND
The Legacy of Kulchur

Introduction

Marcel Smith

I have tried to write Paradise . . .
. . . I botched it.
—Ezra Pound

The writings here assembled, deriving from the Twelfth Annual Alabama Symposium on English and American Literature (October 24–26, 1985), are a variegated lot. And that is quite as it should be. For their subject—the legacy bequeathed to the world by the life and career of Ezra Pound—is itself energetically multifarious. The core of that legacy is perforce controversy. And a cardinal element in that controversy, paradoxical like so much else in it, was Pound's lifelong contempt for most of what calls itself scholarship as practiced in the academic "beaneries" (Pound's expression) that call themselves universities. Pound more than once expressed his contempt for what he called "German" scholarship—the making of articles and books by transcribing information from "sources" onto note cards, shuffling the cards, and transcribing the information onto the pages of a manuscript. For Pound, such activity was a travesty of authentic erudition. Authentic culture, he proclaims in *Guide to Kulchur,* begins when "one HAS 'forgotten-what-book,'" a proposition searchingly examined by Michael North in the essay which concludes this volume. This distinction between authentic culture and bogus *Kultur* is an instance of a more basic distinction that recurs repeatedly in Pound between the phony and the authentic, the false and the bona fide. Pound's critics—witness the pages of this volume—have often brought that concept to bear on Pound himself. The legacy of Ezra Pound *is* controversy. And controversy pervades the chapters of this book.

The writings represent a wide range of points of view—in critical vision, in political vision, in admiration for (or animus against) their subject, and in the formal procedures of critical endeavor. Some of the writings are scrupulously annotated, some less so. The Ezra Pound who appears in them manifests a multiple personality, seen sometimes as a "many-minded Odysseus" and sometimes as a shattered madman—with no agreement on the time of shattering. The variety in these essays is thus not unexpected, nor has it been mitigated. To have imposed an arbitrary editorial unity on these writings would have been disingenuous. For the legacy of culture represented by the figure called Ezra Pound, both while he was alive and since his death, is a response to the explosion of a culture into fragments. Whether that explosion was a destructive catastrophe or whether it was a creative big bang, a cosmic mutation announcing a *novus ordo seclorum*, is very debatable. But that it took place—and is taking place—is not.

In this, as in many other respects, Ezra Pound is a special instance of a general case: the case of human beings entranced by a noble vision which they do not wish to have to acknowledge as delusion. In this, as in many other respects, Ezra Pound is the sibling of nineteenth-century figures whom he affected to despise—for instance, Percy Shelley. Like Shelley, Pound wanted to believe that the human species had inherited a priceless legacy, emerging out of the ancient Mediterranean, developing through the Middle Ages and the Renaissance into an Enlightenment which promised that the birthright could be—in time *would* be—freely claimed, according to capacity, by every living soul. This secularization of messianic hope is the essential promise of the Age of Revolution. One of Ezra Pound's cardinal metaphors appropriately derives from the Great Mother archetype: the Earth our Mother is wonderfully bountiful; there is no reason for any of her progeny to be ill fed or ill clothed, ill housed or ill educated, or arbitrarily prevented from realizing their aspirations according to innate capacity. This secularization of messianic hope is the essential promise of the great revolutions, the American first, then the French, which attempted to sweep away ancient abuse and inaugurate true liberty: the freedom to do anything whatsoever that does not harm others. A benignant spirit is abroad; *il buon tempo verrà.* That hope is the Revolutionary Dream—or, as some say, the Great Delusion. What person of good will can this dream *not* entrance? What person of good will cannot wish it—indeed, *will* it—to be true?

Ezra Pound, like Percy Shelley, willed it to be true. Like Shelley, he threw himself from adolescence onward into an intensely active effort to realize the dream. Like Shelley's, his prophetic zeal, his evangelism, has been seen as a form of Satanic pride. Like Shelley, his life ended in baffled disappointment. He saw the Great Mother beaten and robbed by her own children in the process of their beating and robbing one another. And yet, like Shelley, he never relinquished the dream: "It coheres all right, even if my notes do not cohere."

For Ezra Pound the great embodiment of his version of the dream was the Nuevo Mundo, his native land. Even his fiercest enemies acknowledge that Pound was and remained all his life quintessentially American, though he lived more than half of his eighty-seven years abroad. Even regarding biographical data, intense antagonisms exist among the essays collected here. But a certain outline is definite and clear: Ezra Pound was born in 1885 in Hailey, Idaho; he was an only child. At age four he moved with his parents to Pennsylvania, where he grew up in comfort and security, if not in affluence (his father worked for the United States Mint). He attended the University of Pennsylvania and Hamilton College, where he took a master's degree in comparative literature. In 1908 he arrived in Europe, where he resided (except for very brief visits to his homeland) first in London, then in Paris, and then for twenty years in northern Italy, until he was arrested and charged with treason in 1945, charges deriving from a series of radio broadcasts delivered from Rome in which Pound vigorously opposed American involvement in the Second World War. Declared insane and never brought to trial, Pound was committed to St. Elizabeths Hospital in Washington, D.C., and was kept until 1960. During his incarceration there, St. Elizabeths became a kind of Mecca for writers from all over the world who came to speak with the persecuted genius/infamous traitor, who continued to write poems and prose and letters in support of his version of the Revolutionary Dream. Released after fifteen years of detention, thirteen of those years in St. Elizabeths—and still charged with treason—Pound returned to Italy, where in 1972 he died in exile. During the last decade of that exile, he lapsed into an enigmatic silence, saying of his life's work, "I botched it." It does not follow that he had in fact done so.

One of the many ironies in his career is that as early as 1913—1913!—Pound published in England a series of pieces called *Patria mia*, in which he foresaw an American risorgimento that would make the quattrocento look like a tempest in a teapot. It would include the essential elements of the best that had been thought and said in the world since Sappho and Homer. It would manifest itself not only in literature but also in painting, sculpture, architecture, and music. America at the moment inhabited the Dark Ages. But the promise, the promise. . . . What was wanted was vision and leadership, which he tried to provide. A cardinal element in Pound's vision, another link with the nineteenth century both in England and in the United States, was his axiomatic faith in a class of *aristoi*. Individuals are *not* equal in genius or in discipline; the captains must lead troops, who must follow. After The Great War had burst like a carbuncle over the world, Pound set himself, he says, to "search out the causes of war to oppose same." His search took him to Confucius as the archetypal leader, the benevolent and magnanimous ruler who cared for the people and governed by radiating outward from his cardinal presence a harmonizing order; Pound's archetypal Judases became the Rothschilds, personifications of international finance, and the Schneider-Creusots, armaments manufacturers who sold arms to both sides—incarnations of *cupiditas*, without loyalty to family or to nation, motivated only by a ruthless will to power, a rapacious sodomizing lust.

Of course Ezra Pound did not get his renaissance. He got instead the First World War, which seems to have sneaked up on his blind side. The Great War, the War to End All Wars, functioned in fact as the preamble to the Second World War, which at Hiroshima blew the Industrial Age away and inaugurated the Thermonuclear/Electronic Age, in which the "kulchur" Pound dreamed of preserving and transmitting and enriching has ceased to exist. It inaugurated also his years as an accused traitor incarcerated in a hospital for the insane.

Looking backward now almost eighty years, we may see another dreadful and wonderful irony. Pound arrived in—some say, swaggered into—London in 1908 and commenced to gather the limbs of Osiris, to strive to resuscitate the dead art of poetry, receiving wisdom from Ford Madox Ford, passing it along to W. B. Yeats. He took, it seems, no note (why should he? how could he?) of the culture-shattering implications of the fact that in 1908 the first Tin Lizzie rolled off the first automotive assembly line, a spermatozoon on its way to beget a brave new world.

In 1908, just five years after Kitty Hawk, Pound, like most other humans on the planet, lived and moved and had his being in a world more like London in 1608 than like London in 1918. But in little more than half a century, the first human being would walk on the surface of the moon, and normal human life in the civilized world would be unthinkable without electricity. As Aldous Huxley a few years later recognized, Henry Ford was the archetype of the Nuevo Mundo: a man devoid all his life of anything Ezra Pound would recognize as culture, the progenitor of Wal-Mart and McDonald's and Kentucky Fried Chicken, of Woodstock and Live Aid and the Crystal Cathedral and the shopping mall—of a culture that Flannery O'Connor once characterized in her plantation southern dialect as "the pro-liffa-ray-shun of the soopah-mahket."

At issue here is not whether the proliferation of the super-market is desirable. The point is that the supermarket does proliferate—twentieth-century culture is a shopping mall with the Sears Financial Network as its flagship—and that the culture Pound sought to preserve and transmit and enrich exists today only in unheeded splinters embedded in the minds of a lonely few. His dream of a renaissance blew up like a firebomb in his face.

Someone has written that John Milton (1608[!]–1674) was the last European who had read all the books. It is conceivable, though very unlikely, that John Milton, the last of the Titans, could have read all the books extant at that time on the Euro-pean portion of the planet. By the time Ezra Pound arrived in London in 1908, no one *could* read all the books, even those in English alone. The impossibility is even more prodigious in the 1980s. One does not have to look at a current edition of *Books in Print*. One does not have to look at a current edition of the MLA *Annual Bibliography*. One can look only at a current issue of the *New York Times Book Review*: no one today can, with the best will in the world, identify the best that has been thought and said in the world. Of books and many words indeed there is no end. And if somebody *could*, how could somebody else know that somebody *had*? Unless one knows the difference between a motet and a madrigal, a sonnet and a sestina, one has no way of judging whether anybody else knows. One can, at best or worst, become a true believer in some alleged evangel.

The university itself has become a department of the supermarket, as has the making of books—witness the Norton anthologies in their frequent revisions. In universities not only have the several departments become cells that are cohabiting incommunicado, evaluated by accountants poring over balance sheets; each department is a cluster of persons who do not read the same books. How many professors of literature, for example, have read, in any translation, a complete *Odyssey*, a complete *Metamorphoses*, a complete *Divina commedia*? How many "specialists" in T. S. Eliot or Ezra Pound, carefully poring over *The Waste Land* or *The Cantos*, have read *Les fleurs du mal* in French or have listened to *Tristan und Isolde* in German? Who can claim to have read *The Waste Land* or *The Cantos* or *Ulysses*? Who can validate—or invalidate—such a claim?

Scholarly activity—should the phrase be put in inverted commas?—today has perforce become a rampant cancer; scholars are encouraged, indeed, obliged, to publish, the more the better. Books are better than articles. Value in scholarship becomes like value in clothing or hairstyles or automotive design—a question of fashion and publicity. Just now, on the Exchange, Critical Theory is very hot—as are, in the over-the-counter markets, Lionel Richie and Stephen Spielberg. Jacques Derrida is up five-eighths, Cleanth Brooks down two and one-quarter. And Smith Barney is hard at work trying to foresee the coming trends.

Ezra Pound's career and legacy emblematize these considerations. He is a voice crying in the wasteland, an Ezekiel lying first on one side, then on the other, in front of the doomed Jerusalem, enacting parables which are simply stepped over by the merchants and the police going in and out of the city, until he becomes such a pest that the authorities try to destroy him. Ezekiel in the twentieth century would certainly have been housed at St. Elizabeths—or summarily executed for treason. "The Truth cannot be told so as to be understood and not be believed." Indeed.

Ezra Pound thus remains after his death what he was during his life: a vortex of energetic controversy. That controversy is very much evident in these pages. Among many matters debated, four are cardinal: the claim (made by Pound himself as well as by others for him) that he was *polumētis*, the "myriad-minded Odysseus" whose patroness was Athena, goddess of wisdom, guiding him on his journey toward home again; the validity of the "ideogrammic," or "ideogrammatic," method by means of which Pound claims to organize and unify *The Cantos*, which many readers have found impenetrably complex; Pound's obsessive concern for economics and his insistence that "usura" was the root cause of war among nations; and Pound's anti-Semitism, rooted in his claim that the archusurers were Jews. On these matters, and on others, writers of eminence take opposing positions. Some of them argue that Pound was a great poet and a great man, the magnanimous promoter for the commonweal of other worthy talents who might never have been recognized without his aid. Others portray him as a duplicitous bigot, a treasonous Fascist, and a ruthless womanizer. Some see his reputation as unduly in decline because he is misunderstood and his behavior unjustly distorted. These supporters might paraphrase Mark Twain, who, writing about Fenimore Cooper, observed that it seemed hardly fair for eminent critics to deliver opinions of a writer's work without reading some of it. Others say that Pound does not deserve the respect he has received; he should be dragged, like Shelley's Jupiter, into the depths of the abyss.

What is one to do in the face of such clangor? One may—it is, after all, indeed an option—read Ezra Pound for oneself, according to the proverb, You cannot get fat watching someone else eat. As Pound himself says in "Religio; or, The Child's Guide to Knowledge," there exist only two kinds of knowledge: immediate knowledge and hearsay. And what is the value of hearsay? It tells us to be ready to look.

Though Alfred Kazin in the opening of his essay speaks of the many volumes of Pound's work, the Pound corpus—the torso, anyway, of the corpus—is not in fact very large. (Voltaire's corpus is large.) The Pound corpus is very diverse, as Donald Gallup's meticulous bibliography demonstrates, and because of that diversity it *seems* large. Much of it appears and reappears in a variety of different packages, on a variety of different menus, so that scholarly fervor has plenty with which to keep itself warm. Pound, like his friend Joyce, has become the basis for an enormous and bustling industry. But a stranger to Pound, whether scholar or not, someone who has heard (via, for instance, books like this one) about this famous/infamous genius/madman and who wants to know the man's work at first hand—such a stranger does not have a steep stairway to climb. The trunk of the corpus, easy to get to, consists of two books of verse and half a dozen compact books of prose. Friends introduce friends to friends in a variety of ways. If I were introducing a friend to Pound, I would say, Start with *Personae*, go then to *Selected Prose*, then to the *Guide to Kulchur*, and then, unhurried, to *The Cantos*. Take plenty of time meandering through *The Cantos*, as if strolling through the heart of Paris or London. Expect to see much that baffles, much even that offends—like generic public housing—and, I'll bet, much that magically enchants (the passages, for instance, that Kazin as it were grudgingly cites). If the new acquaintance then desires warmer intimacy, it is easy to find a way to go on.

What, again, is the value of hearsay?

It tells us to be ready to look.

As a sip of wine will tell someone whether or not to finish a bottle, so a stanza or a paragraph may tell someone whether or not to finish a poem or an essay. Pound's friend Eliot somewhere observes that one may be moved greatly by poems one does not at all at first understand. Some persons report that

kind of response to William Blake, Percy Shelley, Arthur Rim-
baud, Walt Whitman, Wallace Stevens—and Ezra Pound: "I do
not know *what* is going on here, but *something* surely is." When
one enters a stanza or a paragraph, one enters a mind—or the
apparition of a mind—bona fide or not. The quality of that
mind may lead one to seek other experiences with it. Or not.

So too with the essays here assembled.

1

Simplicities

Hugh Kenner

In August 1925, in his fortieth year, Ezra Pound, in Italy, seated as usual before a machine, was sending off to America for photographs of machinery. His father, Assistant Assayer at the Mint in Philadelphia, responded with a photo of the Medal Press in the Royal Mint of England. Ezra called the picture "magnificent" and instantly wondered, "Why can't the Uncle Sam mint do something as good in the way of photos of its internal workings?" A good question: it was like the questions he'd long been asking about the poetry they printed in the *Atlantic*. As every visitor to Philadelphia knows, what the Uncle Sam Mint has for sale is celebrations of its exterior encasement, much as what magazines had on display was the look of the sonnet. Soon Ezra Pound was reflecting that a government headed successively by Wilson, Harding and Coolidge wouldn't know that the Mint had any insides.

He has not been alone in remarking American incuriosity about machines and processes. A quarter century later Sigfried Giedion, the Swiss historian of technology, was expressing amazement that the Ford Motor Company had no records of the mass-production techniques it had pioneered, no photos or working drawings of its assembly-line machines. Rather than preserve these documents, Henry Ford had elected to restore Greenfield Village, a kind of museum of procedural archaisms. By contrast, the Kensington Science Museum, a short walk from where Ezra Pound had lived in London, shows you auto-mata that spun and pounded inside Victorian factories. British antiquarian sentiment finds these as interesting as Ezra found the Royal Mint's coin press. For though they like to say they are a literary people, the English are not; they are a technological people. They pioneered the Industrial Revolution, and they understand its poetry. It is only their poets who do not under-stand it.

The English photo was just the kind of thing Pound was looking for. "The NOSE of the big die, for example, excellent shape. Photos of the detail of the coin press, especially at the point where force is concentrated. NOT the damn detail of the *coin*, sentimental symbolism. Miss Murphy the Belle of the Bowery. Liberty before she was lost."

For it was perfectly clear that the face on the coin was some random American face that had caught some depictor's atten-tion. Artists pick faces at whim; the Pre-Raphaelites had picked shop girls. Long before, in Greece, a coin could offer the profile of a goddess. But by 1915, when the U.S. Mercury dime and Liberty half-dollar got designed, artists were willing to let their eyes get caught by "Miss Murphy," the girl next door. So by 1925, Ezra Pound was finding the coin press more interesting than the coin. It contained, he said, "the point where force is concen-trated." And that point was no longer to be found at the tip of the sculptor's chisel.

It is to be found in the innards of a machine, a machine that was the product of an era when you could still understand how machines worked by watching them. The great left arm of a linotype swinging down to collect its used matrices is some-thing you can see, and how they get sorted into the troughs they came from is not mysterious at all as you watch it happen. Such purposeful ballet was not encased; the encasement of machines began in the 1930s, under the rubric "streamlining," which was advertised as a formula for enhancing efficiency and was actually a program for concealing the evidence.

But before that, when the coin press was a visual guide to its own workings, the mind of the machine could be focused on a point of exquisite concentration. Into that space a new blank is slid; next the nose strikes down with a force that embosses the blank on both sides. Then the nose is withdrawn, while a new blank replaces the new coin. In the vicinity of that point of impact everything happens. So, 23 October 1925:

> The good forms are in the parts of the machine where the energy is concentrated. Practically NO machines show high grade formal composition; the minute they hitch different functions, or . . . have parts NOT included in the concentration of the power, they get ugly, thoughtless.

"Parts not included in the concentration of the power": that rhymes with the second clause of the 1914 Imagist Manifesto: No Unnecessary Word. And note the phrasing, "They get ugly, thoughtless": beauty is attention, beauty is incarnate thought. Ugliness, the absence of beauty, is not perversity but lack of thought. It is when a poet isn't thinking, when he's filling out for instance the rhyme scheme of a sonnet, that his work grows empty, ugly. That is also what happens when a designer is specifying the parts his machine needs just to hold it together. Pound had cut *The Waste Land* by removing the lines in which Eliot could be seen filling out a scheme. Those were lines in which energy was not being concentrated.

And his letters about the coin press reaffirm the Vorticist affirmation of 1914:

> The vortex is the point of maximum energy.
> It represents, in mechanics, the greatest efficiency.

> We use the words "greatest efficiency" in the precise sense—
> as they would be used in a text book of MECHANICS. . . .
> Every conception, every emotion presents itself to the vivid
> consciousness in some primary form.
> It is the picture that means a hundred poems, the music that
> means a hundred pictures, the most highly energized state-
> ment, the statement that has not yet SPENT itself in expression.

Hugh Selwyn Mauberley's "urge to convey the relation / Of
eye-lid and cheek-bone / By verbal manifestation" was an urge
ill-directed. He should have been drawing pictures, but he
fussed his energies away. Energy, efficiency, concentration; and
two other criteria of Pound's were "accuracy" and "imperson-
ality." A tool-and-die maker could underwrite that aesthetic.
And not the least of the nineteenth century's artists were its
artisans, men possessed by a new passion for nonredun-
dancy. A suspension bridge by Isambard K. Brunel can com-
mand more sustained respect than The Idylls of the King. So can a
poem such as Pound's 1912 "The Return," in connection with
which it is helpful to recall a distinction from one of his 1925
letters about machines:

> MUST distinguish between machinery, motor parts, and mere
> static structure. The static structure in machines really part of
> architecture and employs no extra principle. Governed purely
> by form and taste.
> It's the mobile parts, and the parts REQUIRED to keep 'em in
> their orbits or loci that I am interested in.

To attend to a poem is to pay heed to an intricate process, all
in plain view. It has no mysterious designs upon us, no formal
concealments comparable to a streamlined shell, and we are
entitled to see everything that is at work. That is one reason
what we see looks a little diagrammatic. And Pound's ideal
poem would consist solely of "mobile parts" and "parts RE-
QUIRED to keep 'em in their orbits or loci." The parts required
may include the placement of words on the printed page. That

can entail a scribe (we now say, a printer) who can reproduce visual instructions exactly, and a way of creating the poem in one's workroom in a form close to the form in which it will be printed. So "The Return" is an early example of what has become a twentieth-century genre, a poem that could have been composed only on the typewriter.

So we come back again to the machine, and it grows important to ward off misunderstanding. The Industrial Revolution, in its early states, made many people unhappy, and from the Blake of the "dark satanic mills" to the Yeats who linked "mechanical" with "servile"—

> And never stoop to a mechanical
> Or servile shape, at others' beck and call.

—in short, for a span of a century and a half—the word *machine* has been made to connote somnambulism, ennui, misery, and idiot repetition.

But somnambulism and idiot repetition were exactly what Pound saw machines putting an end to. Much work entails much repetition, and a machine should be doing that, while a man takes his leisure. Imagine the labor of inscribing "The Return" by hand, letter aligned with letter the way printing will reproduce it. But a typewriter lets you do it in two minutes. Likewise, as we read toward the end of the 18th Canto,

> And the first thing Dave lit on when he got there
> Was a buzz-saw,
> And he put it through an ebony log: whhsssh, t ttt,
> Two days' work in three minutes.

"Two days' work" on an ebony log would entail many thousand fatiguing mindless strokes with a muscled arm, and it's difficult to argue that a man condemned to such toil is well off.

Before there could be buzz-saws, metallurgists had devised alloyed steel for the blade, and machines to cut teeth around the rim of a steel disk had been imagined and constructed too, and also ways to sharpen each of these teeth, and shafts and bearings and lubricants and tractable sources of power. Pound's most powerful historical vision disclosed glimpses of a continuous imaginative current running through the entire story of mankind, manifested now in one form of activity, now in another. Sometimes he offers this under the figure of an underground religion, its tradition coursing

> from the San Ku
> to the room in Poitiers where one can stand
>   casting no shadow,
> That is Sagetrieb,
>   that is tradition.
> Builders had kept the proportion,
>   did Jacques de Molay
>   know these proportions?
>   and was Erigena ours?
>   Moon's barge over milk-blue water
> Kuthera *deina*
> Kuthera sempiterna
>   Ubi amor, ibi oculus.
>   (Canto 90)

The San Ku, in China, ten centuries B.C., was a three-man council charged by the Emperor with making the world's germinative energies shine forth. The room in Poitiers, some 2,500 years later, is the microcosm of a world suffused by light. Erigena said that all things that are, are lights. And Kuthera *deina*, Kuthera sempiterna, the terrible and eternal goddess of beauty, proclaims the motto, "Where there is love, there is sight."

Pound wove many such chains of continuity; and according to one of them, the nineteenth century—a low time for sculpture (the Albert Memorial), for painting (Watts's *Hope*, which looks despairing) and for poetry (even Swinburne can sound like a stuck needle)—had husbanded like all times its legacy of imaginative energy, but not where the aesthetes were looking;

no, in machine shops and in the tool-and-die works and among the men who conceived the linotype, the typewriter, the rotary press, the sewing machine. He delighted to quote a tailor named Blodgett who had thought sewing machines would never come into general use. *There* spoke the perennial art critic. It was Blodgett's intellectual descendants who'd hooted at the Postimpressionists.

The imagination that had flowed into such contrivances was like the kind that had manifested itself in the verses of Sappho, prizing the swift and the sure and always clear about its aims, and certain of where the energy was to be concentrated. It was preserved in blueprints and metal the way Sappho's had been fitfully preserved on parchment. It economized human toil the way art like Sappho's economized and concentrated human perception, human expression. Leonardo, who painted pictures and wrote sonnets and also designed machines, may have been the last man to understand in his bones how these three activities are unified at their root, and he was hampered by a technology which could not realize his machines. Thus he designed a clumsy bicycle to run on wheels like wagon wheels, for lack of the high-tension steel that might have let him conceive wire spokes. Those metallurgies would eventually flower in Victorian England. One of England's triumphs, aesthetic and practical too, would be the safety bicycle. And just one generation after everyone including Henry James (who took cycling lessons) had been mounted on paired wire-spoked wheels, English imaginations had begun to intuit poems of a similar description: elegant, lightweight, spare, maintaining an equilibrium by virtue of movement. And that was starting to happen just in Ezra Pound's first London decade.

So from 1925 we'll go back to 1910, when Pound was a young man in London, learning from Yeats the stances of a poet, from Ford the discipline of prose, and from the air—gathering, as it were "from the air"—the coming and novel prominence of the short poem, where force is concentrated. He could have come upon that novelty only among the English, still in that generation connoisseurs of Iron Age technology.

Here there's no focal figure—no Yeats, no Ford—just an ambience created by the possibility of a few ill-assorted men meeting. That is in itself an interesting sign. There had been a London where one could meet The Poets—Pope, Gay, Swift, Addison, lesser talents. The Poets moreover were largely in agreement, if not about who was accomplished at any rate about what accomplishment amounted to.

But where were the 1910 poets, and what were they agreed on? Yeats was at 18 Woburn Buildings when he wasn't in Ireland, but wherever you found him he was making a point of being outside the public consensus. Thomas Hardy was away in his big forbidding house at Max Gate near Dorchester, and though a poem of his had led off the first issue of the *English Review*, few thought of him as a poet at all. He had built his big forbidding reputation on the "pessimistic" and "outspoken" novels he stopped writing after 1895. Hardy the poet was "awkward." What he and Yeats may have found to say to each other I have no idea. Other people were known on account of a poem or two. Henry Newbolt had written "Drake's Drum." Arthur Symons had written this poem or that (but after 1910 he was mad off and on). Or there was Edward Storer, whose *Mirrors of Illusion* (1908) contained

Street Magic
One night I saw a theatre,
Faint with foamy sweet, and crinkled
loveliness Warm in the street's cold side.

—remarkable for being the entire poem. Storer spoke of "scattered lines, which are pictures, descriptions, or suggestions of something at present incapable of accurate identification." Yes, "Street Magic" with its "foamy sweet" is poetic in the worst sense. Like many of his generation, Storer thought a poem should be made of yummy words. But he'd glimpsed a poem he wasn't able to write; had seen the possibilities of speed and brevity; of what young James Joyce among classmates in Stephen's Green had used to call, somewhat grandly, the Epiphany.

Such a man repays notice, slight as his talent was, for his witness to the ubiquity of an idea. He talks of "pictures" and "scattered lines" and "suggestions," groping to convey the quality of a poem that shall register some brief experience we don't have words for: a new *kind* of short poem, necessarily short. The importance of this idea consists in the fact that other people had glimpsed it too. Pound would call them, collectively, "the 'School of Images,' which may or may not have existed." Insofar as a "school" existed, it met off and on, most informally, in a Soho restaurant. No manifestos were issued, and what got talked about became public only in part, amid later wranglings about what "Imagism" meant and whose idea it was. But "images" don't define the radical novelty of something like this:

> The after-black lies low along the hills
> Like the trailed smoke of a steamer.

That was found by the biographer of T. E. Hulme (1883–1917), in 1960, among Hulme's notes. It is not an excerpt. It appears to be an entire poem, and if that is a judgment we make with some confidence now, we do so as heirs of those Soho restaurant gatherings. To call it a poem would have been preposterous as late as 1900. But of course we're familiar with Pound's "In a Station of the Metro."

Or consider this, another poem by Hulme:

> Old houses were scaffolding once
> and workmen whistling.

—also unpublished by him; but the six he did publish are almost as short; "Above the Dock" has but four lines. Hulme's poems on the whole do not impress; like Storer he's interesting now for the way he seems to take for granted the autonomy of a poem that is very brief, and is concerned with a single perception. That was new. We are coming to the poem as economical machine—what William Carlos Williams would one day call "a small or large machine made out of words."

If the brevity and the snapshot perception were new, an older necessity was also at work. Perception tends toward inventory, and we note the focus on nouns: houses, scaffolding, workmen. The new short poem would have to turn on its nouns, and somebody would have said "Imagism" if Pound hadn't. "Images" are the things nouns prompt you to think of, such as "Petals on a wet, black bough." And here we are in touch with something profound. Ever since—let's say—the Civil War, the mental habits of England had been displaying a tropism toward the noun.

That *something* began to happen thenabouts, something of poetic import, has been widely agreed; Eliot, for instance alludes to "a dissociation of sensibility." Whatever that was, it was the kind of event no one knew about at the time, much as no one was ever aware of living through the Great Consonant Shift that changed *piscis* to *fish, pater* to *father.* And as we can identify the Consonant Shift, so we may imagine our own great-great-grandchildren speaking of our twentieth century as the time when the Great Verb-Noun Shift consolidated itself after some three hundred years. They may want to relate our poetic upheavals to that.

An early symptom had been Dryden's sense that Shakespeare needed rewriting. There was talk of decorum and of the Unities, but if we examine Dryden's dealings with cadence and line we find him busy at something he was perhaps hardly aware of: unraveling Shakespeare's lines that turn on verbs, reweaving them around nouns. "As for her person," wrote Shakespeare of Cleopatra,

It béggar'd all description; she did líe
In her pavilion—cloth of gold of tissue—
O'erpícturing that Venus where we sée
The fancy outwórk nature.

I've marked stresses selectively—not the meter's obligatory
five per line, but the higher-pitched ones we place to clarify
sense—and they fall on "beggar'd," on "lie," on "o'erpicturing,"
on "see," on "outwork" (with the emphasis on the second sylla-
ble). But when Dryden offers

> . . . Where she, another sea-born Venus, lay,

followed by

> She lay, and leant her cheek upon her hand,

though he has twice maneuvered "lay" to where meter will
stress it, yet "she" and "Venus" and "cheek" and "hand" are
words that get a rising inflection. *She* is a *Venus* (apposition);
cheek is on *hand* (rapprochement); Dryden is an early instance of
a new mind that prefers opposed nouns to single verbs, if only
because a stressed verb lets possibilities hover, unpredictable.
And to the extent that an effect is unpredictable it can feel
uncontrolled, a venture into the random, which isn't Augustan.
   Verbs may take us anywhere: "I see . . ."; anything at all may
follow "I see." But Dryden was accommodating to a taste we
share, a taste for the programmed rather than the fortuitous,
taking its pleasure in planned, not improvised, effects. That
helps explain his interest in dramatic Unities, lacking which we
never know where we'll next be—Rome? Alexandria?—or
whether the next act will shift us to next year. But in short verbal
sequences such as concern us here we may detect a like pre-
mium on forethought, equilibration, engineering, needless to
say, on revision ("A line may take us hours maybe"). To catch our
time's resonance writing must *contrive*, and show off its con-

trivance. "Happiness, too, yes there was that too, unhappily,"
writes Sam Beckett, making "happiness" *foresee* "unhappily."
That was not a spontaneous line. Yeats too served a taste for the
foreseen; ". . . And all dishevelled wandering stars" owes its
mournful weight to our sense of a weighty line conceived and
worked out as a whole: not like Shakespeare's way of letting us
imagine that his speakers are just happening on the next word,
as exhilarated by it as are we.

By 1916 Pound was uneasy; he was drawing attention to
verbs, and welcoming Ernest Fenollosa's assurance that nouns
were degenerate verbs, the verb force still latent within them.
One means of releasing it was the cadence of live speech. "In a
Station of the Metro" seems verbless, but the pause between its
two lines works like a silent verb. It's the moment of awed
surprise, and creates a person present and alert.

Yes, all poetry implies a speaking presence; but by Dryden's
time, rather suddenly, orality had receded, to be recovered as
synthetic orality. If the modern short poem offers speech as its
salient criterion, it must presuppose print even so. For it's *seen*
before it is *said*. In an important way, it comes to our attention as
an artifact of the typewriter and the printing press.

Short poems had tended to be short because governed by a
tune, or because constrained by a set form, like the sonnet.
Even a sonnet is not as short as it looks; Donne once got a slow
apocalypse into a sonnet, a feat Yeats would repeat in "Meru."
The sonnet may also be described as a bag you must fill with
rather more than a hundred words, however few you may need.
But now behold something different: the snapshot poem, as
brief as its occasion, free to stop when it's done because it's
"form" is being contrived ad hoc.

It is here that *vers libre* becomes pertinent. If poetry, in Eliot's
famous phrase, "can communicate before it is understood," it
can also communicate before it is even read. After Milton and
Wordsworth, a sonnet could announce by its look on the page
that like the late Mr. Gladstone it was prepared to *say* some-

thing: that a book was writ of late called *Tetrachordon*, that the world is too much with us. The look of a poem is what communicates first. The look of *The Excursion*, long unbroken columns, says to be braced for heavy rumination, and the look of *In Memoriam*, numbered groups of short stanzas page upon page, says that the dolefulness will go on for some time, though not in a steady wail but in stoical episodes. So the first thing to be modified might be the way a poem looked on the page: if it was brief and its lineation irregular, that would suggest wording shaped by some moment's uniqueness. "Free verse" was called for.

If Everyman thought vers libre a French anarchy like absinthe and the cancan, a few dreamers in London were seeing opportunities. Flint had guessed that the future lay open "to the poet who can catch and render . . . the brief fragments of his soul's music." By August 1909 Hulme was comparing prose to an algebra of Xs and Ys which can go on and on, but poetry to a handing over of sensations bodily, "to make you see a physical thing, to prevent you gliding through an abstract process." Now fragments are by definition brief, and the essence of sensations is brevity. To catch perception on the wing like that you'd not want an interposed formality of tum-tum. If Claude Monet had made pictures of appearances, not of salon directives, English *vers libre* might be a poet's response to Monet.

Hulme's interest in writing poems, never strong, had petered out well before his untimely death. Flint is remembered now for excerpts from his articles. As for Storer, Tancred, Joseph Campbell . . . no one need feel obligated to make an anthology. If all now seem minor characters in another story, the story of Ezra Pound, that does not lessen the value of the milieu they helped create. "And pass on the tradition," Pound wrote long after:

> there can be honesty of mind
>   without overwhelming talent
> I have perhaps seen a waning of that tradition.

They peopled a London long since supplanted by a lesser and a trivializing capital.

Vorticism, when it came in 1914, took everyone by surprise; but Vorticism was right to offer itself as authentically *English*. English industry, Wyndham Lewis proclaimed in *Blast No.* 1, had "determined the direction of the modern world," rearing up "steel trees" where the green ones were "lacking"; British seaports were "RESTLESS MACHINES" of

> scooped out basins
> heavy insect dredgers
> monotonous cranes
> stations
> lighthouses, blazing
>   through the frosty
>   starlight, cutting the
>   storm like a cake.

Blast is a typographic as well as a verbal artifact; with its aggressive starkness we can see what experimentation with *vers libre* and the poetry of the noun had been pointing toward: a poetry comfortable in the world of technology, able to collect its wits in a place as clangorous as a station of the Metro, but more than that, a poetry itself conceived as technology, as a marshaling of concentrations of energy, elegant in its unredundancies. The Pound of 1925 who wanted photographs of machines was clear about the nature of their aesthetic because it had shaped his own.

2

Homer to Mussolini: The Fascination and Terror of Ezra Pound

Alfred Kazin

In the museum of modern literature no figure commands more space than Ezra Pound. Born in 1885 and dying at the ripe age of eighty-seven in 1972, he published his first book of poems in Venice, A *lume spento*, in 1908. My packed shelves hold almost thirty volumes of his writings—the early collected poems in *Personae*; the final one-volume collected *Cantos* of 1970; Pound on *The Spirit of Romance*, on "Kulchur," on Joyce, on the classic Noh Theater of Japan and the Confucian Odes; Pound on *How to Read, Make It New, The* ABC *of Reading*; Pound's literary essays and letters; his translations from the Anglo-Saxon, Chinese, French, Greek, Hindi, Italian, Japanese, and Latin; love poems from ancient Egypt; Sophocles' *Women of Trachis*. There are many more in general circulation.

Not in general circulation these days are the "money pamphlets" that Pound wrote in Italian during the war and that were published in London by Peter Russell in 1950: An *Introduction to the Economic Nature of the United States*; *Gold and Work*; *What Is Money For?*; A *Visiting Card*; *Social Credit: An Impact*; *America, Roosevelt, and the Causes of the Present War*. These works are full of fascinating material not likely to be found elsewhere. Abraham Lincoln was assassinated after making a statement on the currency. Franklin D. Roosevelt was "a kind of malignant tumour, an unclean exponent of something less circumscribed than his own evil personal existence. . . . His political life ought to be brought *sub judice.*" Less difficult of access but definitely not in print is *Jefferson and/or Mussolini: L'Idea Statale: Fascism As I Have Seen It* (1935). The United States Government Printing Office put out the speeches that Pound delivered on behalf of the Axis before and after Pearl Harbor on Italian radio for transmission to the United States. In 1973 Pound's estate threatened legal action against me for quoting from these speeches in a magazine article, but they have been edited by Leonard W. Doob as *Ezra Pound Speaking.*

The literature on Pound is enormous and swells every month. Much of it explains and justifies *The Cantos* by annotating them and reminds me of Joyce saying that he would be immortal because *Ulysses* had given the professors work for more than a century. Pound's fellow poets from Yeats through Tate and Auden to Lowell and Jarrell were often indifferent to *The Cantos.* Yeats was baffled and irritated. Professors have no trouble. I write surrounded not only by reminiscences of Pound by H. D. and William Carlos Williams, by the letters exchanged with his future wife Dorothy Shakespear, by old biographies and a new one, E. Fuller Torrey's *The Roots of Treason: Ezra Pound and the Secret of St. Elizabeths*, by a book on Pound's "distinguished American roots," but also by a spate of still more critical studies—*The Dance of the Intellect: Studies in the Poetry of the Pound Tradition; Blossoms from the East: The China Cantos; Pound and Twentieth-Century Thought; Pound, Vorticism, and Wyndham Lewis; Translation after Pound; Pound and Dante; Pound and John Adams; Fugue and Fresco in Pound's Cantos;* Hugh Kenner's doctoral thesis, published as *The Poetry of Ezra Pound*, with a preface detailing how hard it was once to get people to read Pound intelligently.

Whether people now read Pound more "intelligently" is less

certain than that modernism, which used to make history, has
passed into history. It is indeed a museum, every scrap of which
is now necessary to "Kulchur." Pound was determined to be
famous as soon as he reached Europe in 1908. He is now one of
the dominating names in the history of the century. Artistic
progress is measured in the academy of modernist canons.

Modernism was a historical moment from the end of the
"bourgeois" nineteenth century to its collapse in the era of
totalitarianism. It was not so much a movement as an upsurge
of related energies in those wonderful years of illusion just
before World War I. Pound, forever telling his generation to
"Make It New," called it a disturbance and persuaded us that he
was the center of it. From time to time he allowed the "Reverend
Eliot" to share the limelight. When still in London just before
the war, he mocked "the *deah* English public for not understand-
ing that a troika of Americans"—the third was Robert Frost—
"were making all the trouble." Later, he identified modernism as
a fundamental revolution in consciousness whose social cor-
relatives were Fascism—to the end—and Bolshevism in its
beginnings.

Pound saw parallels between his avant-garde activity and
that of Lenin and Mussolini in the political realm. Mussolini
and Hitler described themselves as artists who performed on
history; the masses were their raw material. Pound said in the
twenties, "Lenin is more interesting than any surviving stylist.
He probably never wrote a brilliant sentence; he quite possibly
never wrote anything an academic would consider a 'good sentence,' but he invented or very nearly invented a new medium,
something between speech and action (language as cathode
ray) which is worth any writer's study." In *Jefferson and/or Mussolini*,
his homage to Mussolini as the perfect ruler, he assigns Lenin a
secondary place only because, Russia not having had a classical civilization, Lenin was not able to conceive Fascism. Being
an artist "in a new medium, something between speech and
action," was Pound's role when modernism lost its vital energy

in the thirties and during the war. Pound, still the disturber, plumped for Social Credit and Fascism. His own conviction, never shaken in extreme isolation, was that he knew many things outside of art because he was an artist.

If ever a person looked The Poet as antagonist of bourgeois civilization (especially in Latin countries, where the beard, the wide-brimmed black hat, the open collar, the walking stick, and the defiant look were familiar at Anarchist congresses), it was Pound in the course of a career always full of uproar. There is very little of Pound's personal life in his poetry; from it you would never guess his relations with Dorothy Shakespear and Olga Rudge. But his self-proclaimed persona is all over it. In a film, "Ezra Pound/American Odyssey," centered on him not long before his death, he is as picturesque as ever, sitting in a gondola, still in his classic get-up replete with walking stick. Venice frames him exactly as he frames himself in Canto 3, sitting on the steps of the customhouse on his arrival in 1908.

When you are not looking at Pound himself in this film, you are looking at Italy, with its sunbaked towers and layers of terraces—Italy, the classic land before Christianity which Pound invoked and celebrated so many times that Italy now seems more an extension of Pound than does his birthplace in Idaho or his youth on the main line near Philadelphia. Pound's genius was that he always took all his associations along with him. He was a natural take-over; when his mind did not, his will did. When Pound and Italy are not on the screen, they are replaced by lyric passages from his work. The effect is extraordinary. Pound's silky lyrics move across the screen as if they came straight from his mind. Filaments, fragments, opaline (as he liked to say) in their perfection, vibrant as air, give back the shock of the natural and elude language. This shock, though it is the story of Pound's life, he of course did not understand until it was too late.

> Bright gods and Tuscan, back before dew was shed.
> Light: and the first light, before ever dew was fallen.
> Panisks, and from the oak, dryas,

And from the apple, maelid,
Through all the wood, and the leaves are full of voices,
A-whisper, and the clouds bowe over the lake,
And there are gods upon them,
And in the water, the almond-white swimmers.

Pound was a genius, not least in his American gift for appro-
priating a land not his own, gods distinctly not in the Protestant
tradition, a language so far out of time that his very need to
impersonate it is as impressive as his ability to do so. He
recorded his translation of the Anglo-Saxon *Seafarer.* You hear a
cultivated, deeply musical American voice, trilling his r's in the
upper-class style of Theodore Roosevelt—an affectation that
died out about the time Pound left for Europe. He recites his
poem to the pounding of a drum at appropriate intervals and is
understandably intense. The well-shaped alliterative consonants following each other in Indian file are themselves
drumbeats:

Bitter breast-cares have I abided,
Known on my keel many a care's hold,
And dire sea-surge, and there I oft spent
Narrow nightwatch nigh the ship's head
While she tossed close to cliffs. . . .

Lest man know not
That he on dry land loveliest liveth,
List how I, care-wretched, on ice-cold sea,
Weathered the winter, wretched outcast
Deprived of my kinsmen;
Hung with hard ice-flakes, where hail-scur flew,
There I heard naught save the harsh sea
And ice-cold wave, at whiles the swan-cries,
Did for my games the gannet's clamour,
Sea-fowls' loudness was for me laughter,
The mews' singing all my mead-drink.

Here, as always when Pound is the lyric poet in a state of
grace—not repeating the same anecdote in *The Cantos* about

Jacques Maritain, not bitching about the failure of the English to appreciate him, not railing at the fall of civilizations that would not have fallen if they had read Confucius and John Adams and the autobiography of Martin Van Buren—you feel, as you do when watching Pound's lacy lines streaming across the screen, that his real genius was to identify with poetry itself, poetry without which people once never went to war, poetry as primal element, kin to nature as prose can never be.

None of Pound's generation in English, the modernists born in the "failure" of the last century and determined to remake the next, caught so rapturously as Pound did, from within, poetry's genius for summoning up the beginning of things, the archaic as inception, the childhood of the race, the ability to look at the world as Homer did, for the wonder of creation:

> God-sleight then, god-sleight:
>> Ship stock fast in sea-swirl,
> Ivy upon the oars, King Pentheus,
>> grapes with no seed but sea-foam,
> Ivy in scupper hole.
> Aye, I, Acoetes, stood there,
>> and the god stood by me,
> Water cutting under the keel,
> Sea-break from stern forrads,
>> wake running off from the bow,
> And where was gunwale, there now was vine-trunk,
> And tenthril where cordage had been,
>> grape-leaves on the rowlocks,
> Heavy vine on the oarshafts,
> And, out of nothing, a breathing,
>> hot breath on my ankles.

Seeing, but especially *hearing*, such words, one gets charged up, relieved for the moment from the unfelt emotions so often published in poetry, poetry too often written by people to whom, evidently, nothing very much has ever happened. The force of Pound's lyricism suggests an extraordinary ability to possess and incarnate his classical reading. From this ability to assimilate, he has imagined as actions words he has taken off the page.

Pound did something amazing: he turned himself into a mythical creature, the poet from ancient times. The bard, the singer of tales, which Pound in his genius for sound felt himself to be, has an understandable affinity with war as his element. Pound was unable to understand a society that had lost all contact with poetry as its great tradition. It actually declined to credit Pound with the sagacity he attributed to *il gran poeta*. More isolated abroad, especially after his removal to Fascist Italy in 1925, Pound's talent for seeing life as literary myth increased each year. He finally understood the vast indifference around him: a malignant conspiracy threatened civilization itself. As the crisis of the thirties broke, Mussolini assumed a role in Europe he never could have assumed before. Pound rallied to him with the same pretentiousness and demonstrated a capacity for intellectual hatred that was his only intemperance. As he was himself a natural hero-worshiper, so he attracted acolytes by the force of his gift and his total fearlessness in instructing the "bullet-headed many" how to read, what to think.

What spellbound the acolytes were feats of association; they set up reverberations in his readers and replaced contemporary realities with a web of learning. There was an extraordinary energy, a driving impulse; poetry was assuming powers lost in the nineteenth century to the great novelists. Pound's forever-bristling style in *The Cantos*—the Browning version he learned early—and his zeal for violent types in the heroic mold (condottiere) from Malatesta to Mussolini reflected Pound's harkening back to martial associations with poetry. Such views were certainly not in the minds of poets contained by personal anguish like Matthew Arnold and T. S. Eliot. Arnold thought that the future of poetry was "immense" because it would ease the shock of Europe's dechristianization. Eliot in his journey

from Prufrock's self-conflict to the healing by sacred places in
Four Quartets practiced poetry as a medium of personal evalua-
tion.

Pound never understood such agony. He was no Christian.
Poetry could still be primitive because "the gods have never left
us." With this attitude he helped to establish modernism as a
fascination with the archaic, the unconscious, its disdain for
the mass, its view of industrial society as nothing but mecha-
nization. He was spellbound by the vision of an earlier world,
supposedly more charged and radiant than ours, truer to the
hieratic world identified with art by conservatives and sought
for society by Fascists. Pound boasted of his "American roots"
that he "could write the whole social history of the U.S. from his
family annals." From Italy in 1944 he defended Hitler and Mussolini by writing, "In 1878 my grandfather said the same things
I'm saying now, but the memory of his efforts has been oblit-
erated."

Pound was unyielding in his scorn for those outside the
magic circle of poetry. The force of his rejections was irresistible
to Southern agrarians before they became Texas Republicans
and to literary critics who had enough to do explaining Pound's
allusions to students who thought Virgil was some American's
first name. Katherine Anne Porter referred to "that falling world
between 1850 and 1950. We have been falling for a century or
more, and Ezra Pound came along at just the right time to see
what was happening." Hugh Kenner wrote,

> "To give over all that": to recover the gods, Pound had called it,
> to free (said Lewis) "faculties older than the fish," to achieve
> (Eliot) "the new, the really new," which should be fit company for
> an Altamira bison, these had been the intentions of their vortex,
> dragging a dark world up into the light, forging an ecumenical
> reality where all times could meet without the romance of time,
> as jewelry perhaps Helen's had hung around Sophie Schlie-
> mann's neck for a photograph to be made by daylight, like
> Dublin daylight. An exactness like an archaeologist's.

Guy Davenport commented that the ancient cultures possessed critical tools superior to ours for analyzing reality.

> Poetry and fiction have grieved for a century now over the loss of
> some vitality which they think they see in a past from which we
> are by now irrevocably alienated. . . . The nearest model for a
> world totally alive with the archaic era of our own culture, pre-
> Aristotelean Greece and Rome. . . . Our sciences begin to ex-
> plain the mechanics of everything and the nature of nothing.

It is funny now to think of how resolutely anti-modern (in
spirit) high modernism felt itself to be—while it expressed
itself, as Pound did, in a telescoping of history and in formally
disconnected images that were distinctly novel. Modernism
arrived with the conquest of space by steamers, automobiles,
and airplanes, and the appropriation of Africa and Asia by
Western powers. If in 1853 Commodore Perry had not anchored
his armed squadron in Tokyo Bay, Ernest Fenollosa would not
have spent the twelve years teaching in Japan that left his literary executor, Ezra Pound, with an addiction to the Chinese
written character. The acceleration that Henry Adams saw as the
essence of modern history has defied all attempts at a science
of history. Speedup is the motor of our century. It seems un-
believable now that the horse was still a basic means of loco-
motion and transport when the airplane was being invented.
Historical drive had by 1890 led William James in his *Principles of Psychology* to recognize a *stream* of consciousness. The
obsession with consciousness as a basic flow intermixing non-
successive periods in a person's memory made it possible for
artists—James was distinctly one of them—to record images
of the external world as a personal re-creation from within
oneself. The crucial words in James's chapter 9, "The Stream of
Thought": "Remembrance is like direct feeling; its object is
suffused with a warmth and intimacy to which no object of
mere conception can compare. . . . So sure as this present is
me, is mine, it says, so sure is anything else that comes with the

same warmth and intimacy and immediacy, me and mine." A student of *The Cantos* may well think that William James was reading Pound's mind when he described such imperial confidence in anything that comes to mind. Actually, William James was reading his own troubled mind, trying to liberate himself by accepting the flow as well as the data of consciousness.

The stream of consciousness gave privilege to the person immersed in that stream. Cubism's juxtapositions justified themselves as rhythmic design. Myth ceased to be folklore personifying natural forces and became the past buried in the artist. "Poetry is the past that breaks out in our hearts" (Rilke). "In using myth, in manipulating a continuous parallel between contemporaneity and antiquity" (Eliot), Joyce's method in *Ulysses* was "simply a way of controlling, of ordering, of giving a shape and significance to the immense panorama of futility and anarchy which is contemporary history."

Modernism was a summoning up, a way of establishing order, with peculiarly up-to-the-minute tools that were too much in the spirit of the age to be recognized as such by those fleeing Pound's "half-savage country" for "the spirit of romance." Pound's tool he still called "poetry." Dante was always in his mind, the unifying figure whose journey through hell and purgatory up to paradise Pound saw as model for his epic journey in *The Cantos*, even when he forgot that it really did not have a similar point. Behind Dante was Virgil; behind Virgil, Homer. Epic was a book as action (always a hope to Pound) unifying a race through the chronicle of its wars, sacred places, and gods.

Did Pound begin *The Cantos* thinking he had the qualifications? Not altogether, but he felt that *he* was this affinity with poetry, with its fundamental tonality as a separate medium of speech. Poetry was literature. In the novel he could recognize only those who prized style above everything or had strictness of intention like Flaubert, James, or Joyce. The social application of the modern novel meant nothing to him. The great voices were authority. "With a day's reading a man may have the key in his hand." In treating the novel purely as art object, he was projecting poetic epic as the only true history.

This point he failed to prove in his inordinate subjectivism. The fascination of Pound's *Cantos* lies in its reflection of Pound's mind: not what he brought together but what he could think of from line to line. We are never so much in *The Cantos* as we are observing a performance. We join Pound's mental flight even when we do not follow his subject matter. As for the "matter," his intentions are no help whatever. Pound's mind was not structural in details but assimilative, lyrical, impatient. After some great passage he was always breaking off to introduce something he had read. Early on he told his father that *The Cantos* would constitute a "commedia agnostica" as against the *Commedia divina*. He liked to stress the analogy of the total work to musical structure, mentioning "subject and response and counter subject in fugue." There were to be three principal elements: "Live man goes down into the world of Dead, The 'repeat in history.' The 'magic moment' or moment of metamorphosis, but through from quotidian into 'divine or permanent world,' Gods etc." (I like that "Gods etc.") He hoped that "out of the three main climaxes of themes, permanent, recurrent and casual (or haphazard), a hierarchy of values should emerge."

This work was to be a *modern* epic, "a poem including history" that "encompasses not only the world's literature but its art, architecture, myths, economics, the lives of historical figures— in effect, block letters, THE TALE OF THE TRIBE." En route it would encompass sixteenth-century Italian architecture, Provençal lyrics, Confucian politics, medieval economic history— almost a dozen languages. Pound was going to show "ideas in action" and going to show that "things explain themselves by the company they keep."

The "quotidian" never got into *The Cantos*; perhaps there was no actual *life* around him for Pound to report. The Bible, Homer, Dante, and even Milton reflect the day-to-day life of a civilization. The greatest novels of Western civilization, from *War and Peace* to *Ulysses* and A *la recherche du temps perdu*, are easily called epics. Obviously what we get in Pound is something else. Jean Cocteau defined poetry as a separate language. The specialization of consciousness that the Romantics fostered, the journey into an interior world, attains in *The Cantos* the ultimate in self-absorption, as the roller coaster of Pound's mind plunges up and down into a world largely of his reading.

Starting from the *Nekuia*, the journey to the dead in book 11 of the *Odyssey*, we go from an ordered universe and comprehensive values to one in which everything coming apart is held together by the names and quotations flashing out of the stream of Pound's references. A sustaining image is always water, that particular Greek medium. "Ship stock fast in sea-whirl . . . grapes with no seed but sea-foam . . . Water cutting under the keel . . . And the ship like a keel in a ship-yard, / slung like an ox . . . in smith's sling . . . Fish-scales over groin muscles, / lynx-purr amid sea." Pound's ability to make a frieze out of so many quotations, invocations, and imitations, to place an ornamented sculptured band within a cascade, is extraordinary. Who else would have thought of "lynx-purr"? Moving from the sound this phrase makes to the picture, he is so pleased that his lynx is soon "purring" again—and (typically for Pound) with less sense but just as much beauty.

From the outset we are in a world of names, great place-names—Venice, Burgos, Mount Rokky between the rock and the cedars, Ecbatan, Plantagenet England—and of great names in this culture show of a museum through which an expatriate American is directing us. As Pound said in the *Pisan Cantos*, remembering an aunt's travels—what a commentary on the captivity in which he remembered that—"But at least she saw damn all Europe." Now Eleanor of Aquitaine swims before us, now Henry James.

The house too thick, the paintings
a shade too oiled
And the great domed head, *con gli occhi onesti e tardi*
Moves before me, phantom with weighted motion,
Grave incessu, drinking the tone of things,
And the old voice lifts itself
        weaving an endless sentence.

By Canto 8 we are with Pound's favorite art patron and
brawler, Sigismondo Pandolfo Malatesta, a hero to nobody in
Italy but Pound. But to a passionate pilgrim in Europe, Malatesta is a dream, all *action*, a Renaissance mafioso with a *title*.
By Canto 9, whether as homesickness or as a desire to touch
earth after so much museum fatigue, we get Pound's self-par-
odying American colloquialism, "speech of the tribe" all right:

        "speak humanely,
But tell him it's no time for raising his pay."
. . . .
        Did he think the campaign was a joy-ride?
And old Wattle-wattle slipped into Milan
But he couldn't stand Sidg being so high with the Venetians.

Later we get "pot-scraping little runt Andreas Benzi, da Siena."
Italy to China now. The Great King known to the barbarians as
Confucius. Confucius say,

        If a man have not order within him
He can not spread order about him;
And if a man have not order within him
His family will not act with due order;
        And if the prince have not order within him
He can not put order in his dominions.

Confucius, no Christian he, "said nothing of the 'life after
death.'" Pound, for all the wisdom of the East, does not tell us
that Confucius was deemed impractical and not given office.
    By Cantos 14–16, we are in hell with the English, who are

there for demoting Pound after an excited curiosity about him
and for war profiteering. Proper names have been removed by
the publisher, as they will be in Canto 52 about Jews in "the
international racket."

> The stench of wet coal, politicians
> ——e and ——n, their wrists bound to
>   their ankles,
> Standing bare bum,
> Faces smeared on their rumps,
>   wide eye on flat buttock,
> Bush hanging for beard,
>   Addressing crowds through their arseholes,
>
> Addressing the multitudes in the ooze,
>   newts, water-slugs, water-maggots,
> . . . .
> Profiteers drinking blood sweetened with sh-t,
> . . . .
> And the betrayers of language
> . . . .
> the perverts, the perverters of language,
>   the perverts, who have set money-lust
> Before the pleasure of the senses.

Even the sky over Westminster is greasy. Writers, journalists,
politicians, and press lords are all commingled in

> The slough of unamiable liars,
>   bog of stupidities,
> . . . .
> the soil of living pus, full of vermin,
>   dead maggots begetting live maggots.

We will meet maggots again in the *Pisan Cantos*—Italians who
dared to kill "Boss" Mussolini and his girl Clara Petacci and
hang them head downward from a garage in Milan (adding
insult to execution, for Fascism was born in Milan).

Cantos 31 and following shift to America as the classical republic. T. S. Eliot, when fully settled in London, explained that America had gone under ever since Andrew Jackson replaced John Quincy Adams. Eliot, not as illogically it might seem, made a point on the anniversary of Richard III's death by wearing a white rose. Pound was becoming so hipped on the currency question that he never saw the difference between John Quincy Adams and Jackson's successor and ape, Martin Van Buren. Pound had written before *The Cantos*, "I have beaten out my exile." Coming from a "half savage country," Pound felt he would redeem it by going abroad. But he had been abroad from the time he fell in love with Latinity and explained, "You cannot learn to write by reading English." As the political sky over Europe grew menacing, he fastened on (selected) Founding Fathers as more authority. From miscellaneous reading he shrilled to his private hell anyone he had sized up as an opponent on the currency question. One of his money pamphlets suspected Alexander Hamilton of being Jewish because Hamilton reminded Pound of Disraeli.

Writing about Jefferson and his epoch, Pound sought as always to be the historical dramatist. No one knew better how to pull the best lines from his reading. No one so adroitly shifted and mixed the great voices of the past. Eliot in *The Waste Land* was haunting when he gave us a collage of actual voices. Thanks to Pound's famous cutting, the poem sustains different moods and builds up to a denouement that leads us to expect the actual fall of civilization. Pound the master critic, the great practical critic, cut *The Waste Land* in a way that would have sent him screaming if anyone had proposed equal measures for *The Cantos*. (Such editing would not have worked in any event; the poem is too diffuse.) In the American history cantos, beginning with Canto 31, Pound simply cannot tear himself loose from his reading. And with his *idées fixes* about the influence of credit and the dominance of usury in modern economic life, he kept emphasizing every old quote he could dig up that pointed significantly in the direction of his wisdom—Ezra the giant killer of economics, the Hercules cleaning out the stables.

Pound's genius for the sound and arrangement of words that bring out the *inherency* of poetry did not extend to ideas. In his intellectual rage he was incapable of making the most elementary distinctions. Jefferson as president was forced to declare an embargo on American shipping during the Napoleonic wars in order to keep us from getting embroiled with both England and France. This measure was so unpopular in New England that secession was considered. Fascist Italy had so many unemployed that Mussolini attempted an embargo on emigration. Pound likened Mussolini to Jefferson because both employed an embargo.

Pound was rapturous about leadership, thought everything he saw in Europe the great museum came from the top down, and so, inter alia, enthroned the Adamses as the emblem of administrative genius. Details about the American experience escaped him. Rapallo is a very pretty town on the water but not in the main line even of European communications. Pound built up William Woodward's biography of Washington and Catherine Drinker Bowen's biography of John Adams as the last word on their subjects. He thought that the *Autobiography of Martin Van Buren* had been deliberately kept from the people and never understood that its eventual publication by the American Historical Association was a pious gesture toward a former president who was one of the shiftiest politicians of his day. Pound mistakenly conflated Jefferson with the Adamses, bitter antagonists for the most part. He thought the *Diary of John Quincy Adams* had never been reprinted because of Adams's views on the currency. It is the longest diary ever kept by a public man in America. In transcribing into *The Cantos* quotations from the works of John Adams (Cantos 62–71), Pound reproduced even the misprints in the edition edited by Charles Francis Adams.

Given Pound's equation of the *Führerprinzip* with wisdom and his being so far from home, it now seems inevitable that he should have fallen for Mussolini. Every Italian wall proclaimed *Mussolini ha sempre ragione.* Pound must have been the only inhabitant of Fascist Italy who thought Mussolini always self-possessed. "The Boss," as Pound calls him (because that is what his entourage did), opens Canto 61. This canto is based on Pound's interview with Mussolini, who affably responds to some bright sally, "Ma questo è divertente." Pound seems to have had better luck with the great man than other foreign visitors did. His office above Piazza Venezia was so vast that everyone had to walk an enormous distance to where Il Duce waited with folded arms and the famous scowl of mastership.

But he was The Boss, "catching the point before the aesthetes had got there." What point Pound made is not disclosed. He shifts to:

> Having drained off the muck by Vada
> From the marshes, by Circeo, where no one else wd. have
>   drained it.
> Waited 2000 years, ate grain from the marshes;
> Water supply for ten million, another one million *"vani"*
> that is rooms for people to live in.

The social achievements of Italian Fascism existed mostly on paper. Thanks to the gifted engineer Arrigo Serpieri, the marshes were drained and wheat planted. This step was urgent because there were so many unemployed; Mussolini had no trouble employing thousands for some fifteen years.

This triumph is followed by a story of land speculators put in prison by The Boss, a story told by someone half Jewish, a "mezzo-yit" who is presumably one of the speculators. And now "noi ci faciamo scannar per Mussolini," said the commandante della piazza. The phrase is euphemistically turned around to mean "we would die for Mussolini"—which they certainly did.

In the twenties Pound admitted in a letter to Ford Madox Ford,

> I tried a smoother presentation and lost the Metamorphosis,
> got to be hurley burley, or no one believes in the change of the
> ship. Hence mess of tails, feet, etc. . . .
>   Re the double words, and rep. of cadence. The suffering
> reader is supposed to have waded through seven cantos al-
> ready; MUST BANG THE BIG BAZOO a bit, I mean rhythm must
> strengthen here if he is to be kept going.

The "Big Bazoo" in the world crisis of the thirties ending in war turned out to be "usura" and the Jews. Allen Tate was unfair when he said that *The Cantos* were not *about* anything. But to "include history," Pound's famous postulate for an epic, is not necessarily to describe it. The fascination of *The Cantos*, circling around golden bits of lyric landscape, lies in the journey up and down Pound's mind, which for great stretches shows mostly his reading.

> I can further say with safety there is not a crowned head
> in Europe whose talents or merits would entitle him
> to be elected a vestryman by any American parish.
>   T. J. to General Washington, May 2, '88.
> . . . .
> . . . or paupers, who are about one fifth of the whole.
>   (on the state of England in 1814).

We read what Emperor Alexander said to John Quincy Adams along the Neva. Sir Basil Zaharoff the arms salesman becomes "Metevsky." Then we have Joyce, Marconi, and Jimmy Walker. August Belmont comes to America to represent the Roths-childs; Field Marshal Hindenburg at a concert is annoyed by the music of Mozart. Better not to ask why Charles Francis Adams appears as Charles H. Adams. Then, since Pound is never out for the count, the great passage—and very beautiful it is—from Canto 45:

With *Usura*
    With usura hath no man a house of good stone
    each block cut smooth and well fitting
that design might cover their face,
with usura
hath no man a painted paradise on his church wall
. . . .
with usura, sin against nature,
is thy bread ever more of stale rags
is thy bread dry as paper,
with no mountain wheat, no strong flour
with usura the line grows thick
with usura is no clear demarcation
and no man can find site for his dwelling.

My pleasure in these deeply felt and beautifully structured lines is somewhat diminished by Pound's fond belief that usury is always a conspiracy against the public by alien forces. In the United States of America in 1985, state legislatures are abolishing antiusury statutes at the behest of banks in the credit-card business and offer employment to states that formerly prohibited banks from operating across state lines. Ordinary economic history interested Pound as little as the fact that Mussolini, despite vast numbers of the unemployed, wanted a 22 percent expansion of the population in order to give Fascist Italy more muscle in the rivalries of the century.

Pound in the midst of his campaign against usura did not forget the rivalries of poetry. Canto 46 opens with the sour admission that Pound's tale of usura "will not get through to the boobs," and if you think it will,

    . . . or that the Reverend Eliot
has found a more natural language . . . you who think you will
get through hell in a hurry. . . .

But we are in hell, for enter the Jews in Canto 52, sound the

drums. Pound has been told that the Hebrew word for usury is
neschek. We cannot make out whose names have been blacked
out on page 257 of the final collected *Cantos*. But it is clear that
somebody whose name ends in *-sin* is "drawing vengeance,
poor yitts paying for a few big jews' vendetta on goyim." This
line is Pound's response to Hitler, whom he was to praise in his
broadcasts as having "ended bad manners in Germany."

"Neschek" for usury, "yitt" for yid. Someone told him that the
Hebrew language contained a word for weapons, *chazims*, which
Pound took to mean knives. Rabbi Ben Ezra, as Conrad Aiken
called him, never could resist sound clusters in a foreign lan-
guage. Pound in this section manages to cover Gertrude Bell,
the famous traveler in the Near East writing to her mama about
England's need to keep its pledge to the Arabs in Palestine.
"Thus we lived on through sanctions," refers to the League of
Nation's farcical protest against Mussolini's rape of Ethiopia.
And so on to

> through Stalin
> Litvinof, gold brokers made profit
> rocked the exchange against gold.

Pound refers to Maxim Litvinof, the Jewish foreign secretary of
the Soviet Union in the thirties, long out of favor even before
Stalin made his pact with Hitler. In his last years, reports his
English wife, Ivy Low, Litvinof expected arrest and slept with a
gun under his pillow.

Through "Stalin Litvinof" (presumably the same person)

> . . . gold brokers made profit
> rocked the exchange against gold
> Before which entrefaites remarked Johnnie Adams (the elder)
> IGNORANCE, sheer ignorance ov the natr ov money
>   sheer ignorance of credit and circulation.
> Remarked Ben: better keep out the jews
>   or yr/ grand children will curse you
> jews, real jews, chazims and *neschek*
> also super-neschek or the international racket.

(The rest of this section is blacked out.)

A dozen or more lines down Pound eases into one of his beautiful lyrics,

> The green frog lifts up his voice
> and the white latex is in flower.

But when Pound's mind operated at full stream under the pressure of his many hatreds, he uttered one of the most frightful lies yet perpetrated about the Holocaust. The "poor yitts"—dismissed, exiled, imprisoned, tortured, massacred in Germany, Italy, France, Belgium, Holland, Greece, Norway, Denmark—are paying for the crimes of Jewish bankers. Hitler told the Reichstag in 1939 that the Jews would be massacred if "they" started the war. Pound pretends to sympathy for the "poor yitts," but unlike Hitler, he believes his own atrocity stories.

And now we have arrived at the *Pisan Cantos*. The war is over, and Pound in his cage is sorrowing over

> The enormous tragedy of the dream in the peasant's bent
> shoulders
> Manes! Manes was tanned and stuffed,
> Thus Ben and la Clara *a Milano*
>   by the heels at Milano
> That maggots shd / eat the dead bullock
> DIGONOS, . . . but the twice crucified
>   where in the history will you find it

At this point it would be funny to play Professor X and confront "this text for itself alone," history being extraneous to literature (still!), except as literature like Pound's itself writes the history. But we cannot depend on Pound to describe rationally Mussolini's ruin and his own as he sits in a cage at the United States Army's Disciplinary Barracks outside Pisa, writing these lines on a table made for him by a black soldier awaiting execution.

In his portraits of the duke and duchess of Urbino, Piero Della Francesca included their landscape. How I wish someone could have painted Pound against the Italian landscape in 1943–45 as he sat writing that beautiful much-cited passage,

> What thou lovest well remains,
> the rest is dross
> What thou lov'st well shall not be reft from thee
> What thou lov'st well is thy true heritage
> Whose world, or mine or theirs
> or is it of none?

What a landscape with figure that would have been! Italy in ruins, hundreds of thousands of soldiers dead in Sicily, Calabria, Crete, Greece, and Russia. Of the fifty thousand Italian Jews before the war (one for every thousand Italians), less than thirty thousand will be found in Italy at war's end. In this least anti-Semitic country in Europe, among people who still called Jews "ebrei" (Hebrews), 13 percent have emigrated and 12 percent have accepted conversion (often the price for being harbored by the Vatican). Out of the 8,360 deported to Auschwitz, 7,740 are dead. Among Italy's leading exiles were Toscanini, Salvemini, Silone, and Modigliani. Matteotti was murdered early in the regime, Gramsci was allowed to leave prison for a clinic because he was dying. Mussolini had ordered, "This brain must be stopped from working."

Europe, Pound's great good place, was everywhere in ruins. Yet Pound until his capture was blissfully out of it. He visited Mussolini's "Republic of Salo" on Lake Garda, ringed by the Nazis who delivered him from a penal island. Pound even spouted his economic nostrums to Italian Fascists, who must have thought him crazy not to be aware that the "social republic" was a joke and that Mussolini was doomed by the hatred of his people. Of course we are dealing here with some remarkably self-centered types. Mussolini was pouting that he would never go back to Rome, wanting to punish the ungrateful people for celebrating his ouster from office in 1943. Pound, despite warnings from friends, insisted on broadcasting Axis propaganda after Pearl Harbor and, says Torrey in his book on Pound in St. Elizabeths, volunteered to broadcast in Hitler Germany. He never understood—or did he?—that what from his mouth would be excused by other writers could be understood by ordinary folk as encouragement to murder. At one point he chortled about "fresh meat on the Russian steppes." On April 3, 1942, he called for a "pogrom at the top. . . . But on the whole, legal measures are preferable. The 60 kikes who started this war might be sent to St. Helena as a measure of world prophylaxis, and some hyper-kikes or non-Jewish kikes along with them."

In St. Elizabeths, talking to Allen Ginsberg and invoking his old friendship with Louis Zukofsky, Pound charmed his audience with the disclosure that his anti-Semitism was "a suburban prejudice." Bewitched by words as usual, he also explained that no one named Ezra could really be anti-Semite. Whether or not he always knew what he was saying—clearly impossible in such a lifetime's flood of words—Pound was dishonest, and so were his defenders, when he finally claimed insanity as a reason for his actions. He got away with it.

Pound was a convinced Fascist. The cruelty and death of Fascism are an essential part of his epic and cannot be shrugged away in judging his work. Pound recognized his epic hero in Mussolini because Fascism, like Ezra Pound, had few abiding social roots and was based on an impersonation, like Pound's, of a mythic personage. Pound was a racist, a defender of racial persecution, indifferent to the obliteration of fellow artists. These aberrations were not personal but part of hierarchical beliefs into which he grew through long years of alienation from his country and from the people around him. Pound was a Fascist in a period when everything turned against the humane spirit of pre-1914 Europe in which modernism began.

The growing tendency of our century is against the spirit.

Nowhere is it more striking than in the museum of modern literature, where the curators of the modernist classics replay their authors as Pound replayed the epic poets. In the masterpiece of the Pound industry, *The Pound Era*, Hugh Kenner offers a defense of Pound's anti-Jewish writing and activity along the following lines. The Rothschilds defeated Napoleon. They were despised outsiders who sought to dominate and use those who had snubbed them. Such Jews resemble Sir Basil Zaharoff, the international arms salesman born in Turkey of Greek-Russian parentage, who is said to have hated the British all his life because a Britisher kicked him in Constantinople. Strangely, Zaharoff established a chair at Oxford and was knighted. Kenner notes, "Hitler jailed no Rothschilds."

I have never been as interested in the Rothschilds as Pound was, but Pound's suggestion that "poor yitts" were paying for the crimes of the Rothschilds, which Hugh Kenner picks up, led me to look up the history of the family during Hitler's war. Elie and Alain de Rothschild were on the Maginot Line and became prisoners of war. Louis de Rothschild was a hostage. Guy fought with the Free French. Phillippe was arrested by Vichy at the request of the Nazis and eventually made his way to Spain, whence he climbed the Pyrenees to join the Free French. Edmund was an artillery major in the Italian and North African campaigns. Colonel Victor Rothschild was an intrepid bombremoval expert, whose work earned him the George Medal from England and the United States Bronze Star and Legion of Merit.

Pound, in Kenner's words, thought that "the poor Jews whom German resentment drove into concentration camps were suffering for the sins of their inaccessible religionists."

> Stinkschuld sin drawing vengeance, poor yitts paying for
>   Stinkschuld
> paying for a few big jews' vendetta on goyim

This lunatic thesis is Pound's. But what is Professor Kenner up to? "It is a pity that Pound's distinction between the financiers and the rest of Jewry was not allowed to be emphasized while he was still in the habit of making it. Correctly or not, it attempted a diagnosis, and one tending rather to decrease than to encourage anti-Semitism." Kenner then defends Pound on the grounds that in 1938, when Pound wrote those passages, the concentration camps were "not yet committed to a policy of extermination. News of that policy, when it was instituted, no more reached Rapallo than it did most of Germany."

To mark the fortieth anniversary of V-E Day, the president of the German Federal Republic, Richard von Weizsacker (his father was indicted for war crimes) addressed the Bundestag on the subject of "Hitler's Legacy":

> At the root of the tyranny was Hitler's immeasurable hatred against our Jewish compatriots. Hitler had never concealed this hatred from the public, but had made the entire nation a tool of it. Only a day before his death, on April 30, 1945, he concluded his so-called will with the words, "Above all, I call upon the leaders of the nation and their followers to observe painstakingly the race laws and to oppose ruthlessly the poisoners of all nations: international Jewry." Hardly any country has in its history always remained free from blame for war or violence. The genocide of the Jews, however, is unparalleled in history.
>
> The perpetration of this crime was in the hands of a few people. It was concealed from the eyes of the public, but every German was able to experience what his Jewish compatriots had to suffer, ranging from plain apathy and hidden intolerance to outright hatred. Who could remain unsuspecting after the burning of the synagogues, the plundering, the stigmatization with the star of David, the deprivation of rights, the ceaseless violation of human dignity? Whoever opened his eyes and ears and sought information could not fail to notice that Jews were being deported. The nature and scope of the destruction may have exceeded human imagination. But in reality there was, apart from the crime itself, the attempt by too many people, including those of my generation, who were not to take notice of

what was happening. There are many ways of not burdening one's conscience, of shunning responsibility, looking away, keeping mum. When the unspeakable truth of the Holocaust then became known at the end of the war, all too many of us claimed that they had not known anything about it or even suspected anything.

The contrast between what history knows and what Pound thought he knew threatens the integrity of literary study if it reduces itself to apologia and to vicarious scorn for what the modernist masters scorned. Ever since modernism became academically respectable, it has threatened to take over the curriculum. Eliot's prescription—past literature constantly being assimilated to the taste of the present—has led to a steady omission and distortion of actual history. Modernism must not become the only writer of its history, especially when puffed up with the antidemocratic and racist views of Ezra Pound. Modernism is not our only tradition. The museum of modern literature, like all museums these days enshrining the first half of the twentieth century, cannot show us all that we leave out and even deform in the name of art.

3

Nature and Design: "Burying Euclid Deep in the Living Flesh"

Harriet Zinnes

It is one of the hardest things in the world to say anything sensible about works of art at all.

—Pound

I must repeat a story that all Poundians know.[1] Ezra Pound in July 1913 is visiting the Allied Artists' Exhibition at the Albert Hall. He is there with his future mother-in-law, Olivia Shakespear, a onetime lover of William Butler Yeats. Perhaps in his exuberance he is "swinging along," as the American sculptor Nancy Cox-McCormack in her unpublished memoir has written about another occasion, and "like a western maverick, his bronze mane ruffled by the hot August breeze, his red beard, meeting closely clipped side whiskers, pointed belligerently outward over an open, informal blue shirt collar, exposing a graceful throat."[2] Perhaps he is also wearing what Cox-McCormack called on her first seeing the poet a "worn black velvet coat, buttoned from robust chest to the lean hip line ... . trim and neat." He is in the gallery wandering about, as he said later, "hunting for new work and trying to find some good amid much bad," when a young man "came after us, like a well-made wolf or some soft-moving, bright-eyed thing." They played a kind of game, with Pound "playing the fool" and the young man willing to be amused by the performance. It was a warm, lazy day, there with a little serious criticism mixed in with our non-sense. On the ground floor we stopped before a figure with bunchy muscles done in clay painted green. (It turned out to be the sculptor's *Wrestler.*) It was one of a group of interesting things. I turned to the catalogue and began to take liberties with the appalling assemblage of consonants: "Brzxjk——" I began. I tried again, "Burrzisskzk——" I sneezed, coughed, rumbled, got as far as "Burdidis——" when there was a dart from behind the pedestal and I heard a voice speaking with the gentlest fury in the world: "Cela s'appelle tout simplement Jaersh-ka. C'est moi qui les ai sculptés." And he disappeared like a Greek god in a vision.

This "Greek god" was no other than the French artist Henri Gaudier, who had added "Brzeska" to his name to honor the older Polish woman with whom he was living, Sophie Brzeska. That Gaudier disappeared "in a vision" was prophetic, because very soon, on June 5, 1915, this twenty-three-year-old artist, who had anticipated so much in modern sculpture, suddenly in one blast would die—at Neuville St. Vaast, "gone out through a little hole in the high forehead," as Ford Madox Ford poignantly described it. Yet before this lithe, smallish man was gone "after months of fighting," he had twice been promoted for "gallan-try." "His death in action," wrote Pound in his "Preface to the Memorial Exhibition, 1918," "is, to my mind, the gravest indi-vidual loss which the arts have sustained during the war."[3]

Gaudier's death staggered Pound. He began to collect mate-rials for a book about the sculptor. His *Memoir of Gaudier-Brzeska,* published in 1916, has become an important document on Vorticism, the only significant British art movement of the twentieth century. Created almost single-handedly by the painter Wyndham Lewis, named by Pound, who was its chief publicist, and explained best of all by Gaudier in two explosive articles, one written from the trenches, the movement was over almost before it began, cut short by the war and unsupported by art dealers or the British government. There were no Vollards or Kahnweilers for the Vorticists as there were for the contemporary Cubists in Paris.

Gaudier's death changed Pound's views about war. *Blast, the Review of the Great English Vortex*, a "puce-colored monster" that proclaimed to a momentarily startled English elite the emergence of the Vorticist movement on the eve of the Great War, had an almost manic fury—in fact, it was not far from a hate manual, voicing the inchoate belligerent ultraconservatism of both Lewis and Pound and, in the case of Pound, his anti-Semitism. It is hard to read his poem "Salutation the Third," published in *Blast No. 1* in 1914, without remembering Pound's tragic involvement in World War II. But when World War I took Gaudier and the philosopher T. E. Hulme, who influenced Pound's Imagist aesthetics, Pound's hatred took still another turn: he began bitterly to denounce war and the instigators of war—the bankers, who, to Pound, were synonymous with the Jew. In 1920 he wrote one of his major poems, *Hugh Selwyn Mauberley*, containing those unforgettable lines (except ironically forgotten by Pound in his war broadcasts over Radio Rome during World War II):

> There died a myriad,
> And of the best, among them,
> For an old bitch gone in the teeth,
> For a botched civilization,
> Charm, smiling at the good mouth,
> Quick eyes gone under earth's lid,
>
> For two gross of broken statues,
> For a few thousand battered books.

Mauberley not only was Pound's farewell to England (he left for Paris), but it was also his farewell to aestheticism, to the world of Pater, a world where the poet had witnessed "the end of breeding," in which the lady's "boredom is exquisite and excessive." Though his letters show that he felt he had never left Vorticism, he had certainly given up the formalist emphasis of Vorticism, for he now turned to the world of economics, to what he called "the usurers," who, he felt, had caused the war. In 1960, in *Impact*, the poet declared, as he looked back upon the effects of World War I, "Whatever economic passions I now have, began *ab initio* from having crimes against living art thrust under my perceptions."[4] The death of Gaudier and the artist's earlier struggle to devote himself to his art without patronage symbolized to Pound the economic and political crimes that particularly injured artists, helpless against an uncaring state, a greedy financial structure. Pound, deeply affected by the "enormous wrong of this death," wrote his *Memoir*, and turning to economics and history to expose the errors of people and governments, he began earnestly to dedicate himself to *The Cantos*, his "tale of the tribe."

When Pound had met Gaudier in 1913, the poet was twenty-eight years old, an American in London who had already amazed the English not only with his flamboyance but with his knowledge, arrogant even then, of the world—and I emphasize, the world of poetry. He may have been a provincial American in many ways—or what Gertrude Stein called "a village explainer"—but through his own Imagism, his selfless energy in the support of such writers as T. S. Eliot and James Joyce and such artists as Henry Gaudier-Brzeska, he had helped introduce modernism to England.

But what was that modernist art, particularly Gaudier's art? Why was it so appealing to Pound? Gaudier, as the sculptor Jacob Epstein declared, had the power of assimilation. His quick mind (like Pound's) could turn from the influence of Rodin (whom "he had," said Pound, "thank heaven, discarded") to the influence of an Easter Island carver of a gigantic figure he studied in the British Museum called Hoa-Haka-Nana-la from the cult village of Orongo. Like the Cubists, Gaudier was attracted to African geometrics for his modern formulations. Such geometries also appealed to Pound, who argued for "non-representation" in painting, for a respect "not for the subject matter, but for the power of the artist."[5] The poet's demand for an absolute rhythm in poetry was a parallel literary argument.

Hieratic Head of Ezra Pound, 1914, by Henri Gaudier-Brzeska

The influence of primitive art served Gaudier well in his marble bust of Ezra Pound. Pound as sitter spent hours with Gaudier in a dismal studio under the railroad arch in Putney. Despite the incessant noise of trains overhead, Pound wrote in his *Memoir* that "some of my best days, the happiest and the most interesting, were spent in Gaudier's mud-floored studio when he was doing my bust. . . . He was certainly the best company in the world." Pound later felt that, had he lived in the quattrocento, he should have had "no finer moment, and no better craftsman to fill it." And he added this generous compliment from one master about another: "And it is not a common thing to know that one is drinking the cream of the ages."[6]

The bust, now known as the *Hieratic Head of Ezra Pound*, was made from the half-ton block of marble that Pound had purchased for the sculptor. If Pound had not purchased the marble,

Gaudier would have had to execute the head in plaster, the cheapest medium and one that Pound had called "most detestable." The work represents two months' actual cutting and was preceded by a hundred drawings.[7]

Richard Cork argues that the sculptor "kept the Easter Island figure securely in the back of his mind as he disposed the various sections of his carving into their unpredictable format." He suggests that

> if particular similarities between the two images centre on the areas of the eyes and mouth, it appears likely that Gaudier has been inspired above all by the whole vertical identity of the Orongo figure, thrusting its way up into the air in one compact cubic mass of stone. Just as the head of Hoa-Haka-Nana-Ia is wedged on its torso without any regard for the thinner shape of an intervening neck so Pound's face rests on a wide base which exists only to ensure that the outlines of the whole sculpture travel up in one consistent direction towards the wider block of hair at the top. This gives the sculpture a sense of mass, the very aim of Gaudier's work.[8]

The *Head* is not only striking in its arrangement of planes and angles—thus pleasing in its geometries to both the poet and the sculptor—but, as Cork's description suggests, rich in phallic symbolism. The critic says, in fact, that "the overall silhouette . . . succeeds in suggesting a circumcised penis." When one remembers Gaudier's attraction to African and Oceanic cultures and his special praise of the employment in their crafts of sexual symbolism, the phallic motif in the *Head* is not surprising. Sexual exploits, furthermore, were not unadvertised among these macho Vorticists. Only the artist and friend of Gaudier, Horace Brodsky, seems to have found the talk excessive. He noted that "there was too much sex-art talk" among them and recalled that, when he visited Gaudier while the sculptor was working on the *Head*, "Pound had asked him to make it virile and this Gaudier was endeavouring to do, explaining to me the general biological significance." Brodsky went so far as to claim that the *Head's* "purpose and beginnings were entirely pornographic. Both the sculptor and sitter had decided upon that."[9] But perhaps this claim was merely the consequence of Brodsky's animosity against Pound.

On the other hand, as Timothy Materer reminds us in his book on the vortex, it would have been appropriate for Gaudier to shape "his subject in a form that suggests a phallus" because of Pound's theories on the link between sexuality and creative genius. Whatever the sculptor's intentions, however, he did tell his sitter that the *Head* would not look like the poet. Pound understood and wrote later that the bust was made "infinitely more hieratic" than the poet himself. "Oh well," he added, "*mon pauvre caractère*, the good Gaudier has stiffened it up quite a lot, and added so much wisdom, so much resolution. I should have had the firmness of Hote-hotep, the strength of the gods of Egypt. I should have read all things in the future. I should have been a law-giver like Numa."[10] Is Pound using the word *stiffened* in a double entendre? Probably not. He is attributing to the *Head* something sacerdotal, hieratic, something—and here he shows himself uncharacteristically though playfully immodest—lacking in himself.

The poet's last words on the subject of the *Hieratic Head* are filled with tragic irony: "And we joked of the time when I should sell it to the 'Metropolitan' for $5000 and when we should live at ease for a year . . . some two or three decades hence."[11] Gaudier would be killed within two years, and Pound in three decades would be raging in broadcasts from Radio Rome sometimes in gibberish, sometimes in ugly anti-Semitic and totalitarian venom. Ezra Pound, *mon pauvre caractère*, who thought he was voicing the dreams of the American Fathers, the tenets of the American Constitution. Lewis was right: Pound never did have a sense of political realities.

"*Vive La France*," 1914, by Filippo Tommaso Marinetti (Collection, The Museum of Modern Art, New York. Gift of Benjamin and Francis Benenson Foundation)

The magazine B*last*, with its sensational typography, its puce-colored cover, and its large format—a real PR job—was violent, massive, fashionable. It followed the book *Zang Tumb Tuum* (1914), by the Italian Futurist F. T. Marinetti, and the four-page Futurist proclamation *L'antitradition futuriste* (which had appeared in Marinetti's magazine *Lacerba* in June 1913), by Apollinaire, the French poet and defender of the Cubists.[12] The English magazine blasted the self-satisfied Londoners still living in a Victorian age as if industrial England had stood still amid its roaring machines. These English artists, these rebels from the Omega Workshop of Roger Fry, wanted to will English

art into the twentieth century through their own creative energies. Wyndham Lewis, as Pound said, "supplied the volcanic
force" to the magazine, but Pound had named the movement
almost at the moment of the printing of the first issue.

There were only two issues—the blasts of the guns of the
First World War ended the magazine of the "Great London
Vortex." The Vorticists, as Pound named them, were few in
number. Even Dorothy Shakespear, a painter and the wife of
Ezra Pound, though she said that Vorticism "came just as I
needed a shove out of the Victorian," never displayed her work
in their exhibitions. In addition to Gaudier and Lewis, the Vorticists included the painters Frederick Etchells, Edward
Wadsworth, Jessica Dismorr, Helen Saunders, and William
Roberts. Pound, Lewis, and Gaudier contributed Vortex manifestos to Blast No. 1 to explain the aesthetic principles of the
movement. Yet, as Cork notes, the principles "have remained
blurred."[13] It seems to me, however, that they are less blurred
than contradictory, which we should expect among so many
artists. Dorothy Pound, however, understood the aim of Vorticism: it was a radical art movement to turn England from the
sentimentalities of Victorianism and to awaken its artists to a
new aestheticism because of the new industrial realities.

Lewis called for an art that would reflect the machine age,
from which everything would follow: the hard line, clarity of
outline, whirlpools of energy—violent motifs demonstrating
dehumanization. France already had its Cubism, Italy its Futur-
ism, Russia was on the threshold of Constructivism, England
would have its related modernist movement, Vorticism, but it
would attack the static, blurred mechanical imagery of Futur-
ism, its sentimental attitude toward the machine, and its desire
to do away with the art of the past. Unlike the Futurists, the
Vorticists did not want to sweep away art history. Living in an
industrial age, they wanted their art to utilize its imagery. The
contemporary artist would produce contemporary art but
would not have to deny the importance of past art. Vorticism,
however, was not interested in history per se. It was an aesthetic

movement, despite its seemingly sociopolitical origins. Pound was happy to hear Jacob Epstein talk about "form, not the *form of anything.*"[14] A quick summary of the various manifestos of the *Great Review of the English Vortex* may help to support this interpretation.

Gaudier's explanation of the sculptural vortex explodes with the ferment of his beliefs, not so much in Vorticism (although he was one of the major Vorticists, he was actually not concerned with Vorticist polemics), but with the powers and functions of his own aesthetic medium, sculpture. He wrote, in part:

> Sculptural energy is the mountain.
> Sculptural feeling is the appreciation of masses in relation.
> Sculptural ability is the defining of these masses by planes.[15]

What do these words mean? In this description of the rebel British sculpture, there is no mention of representation, the mimetic, nature, or the figurative. There is no mention of a story, of an artist's desire to commemorate or to narrate events. Clearly, Gaudier's chief emphasis is on form. Pound in his *Vortex* in the same issue of *Blast* argues for an appropriate form in all the arts. In his 1912 *Ripostes*, he had already attacked the Impressionists, who, he wrote, had "brought forth: Pink pigs blossoming on the hillside." He was, in his own witty way, indicating his impatience not so much with their subject matter as with the Impressionists' handling of banal forms. The poet found the Postimpressionists equally ridiculous, for they "beseech their ladies to let down slate-blue hair over their raspberry-coloured flanks."[16]

In *Blast No. 1* Pound sets forth his Vorticist formalist aesthetics without the earlier ridicule. He writes that "the vorticist relies on this alone; on the primary pigment of the art, nothing else." Lewis, in defining the movement, retained his opposition to the Cubists and Futurists (but of course without these avant-gardists his own movement very likely would not have been created):

> By Vorticism we mean (a) *Activity* as opposed to the tasteful
> *passivity* of Picasso (b) SIGNIFICANCE as opposed to the dull or
> anecdotal character to which the Naturalist is condemned; (c)
> ESSENTIAL MOVEMENT and ACTIVITY (such as energy of a
> mind) as opposed to the imitative cinematography, the fuss and
> hysterics of the Futurists.[17]

Despite the stress on form in these pronouncements, it is
wrong to assume that Gaudier, Pound, and Lewis (who had
noted in *Blast No.* 1 that "the finest Art is not pure abstraction,
nor is it unorganized life") were urging the English avant-garde
into pure abstraction. Lewis thought Kandinsky was "the only
PURELY abstract painter in Europe." Significantly, Lewis's
"abstract" work does not resemble Kandinsky's, who, at his
best, Lewis thought "wandering and slack" because he "is so
careful to be passive and medium-like, and is committed, by
his theory, to avoid almost all powerful and definite forms." Still
more significantly, Lewis never denied art's relation to nature. It
was always "nature and design." In later writings Lewis attacked
vituperatively artists working in abstraction because they rejected forms rooted in life. In *Blast No.* 2 he stated that to
"attempt to avoid all representative elements is an . . . absurdity," and again, "everything is representation, in one sense,
even in the most 'abstract' painting"[18] Only in the brief Vorticist
period of 1914–15 did Lewis repudiate obvious representation,
and even those so-called abstract canvases usually reveal aspects of a figure—a leg, a face, a body arching, an organic
contour, a machine form. Gaudier, for his part, intended to write
an essay on the need for organic form, which was left unwritten
because of the blast of a gun.

Pound's Vortex manifesto explains the literary vortex. A
vortex, the poet wrote, "is the point of maximum energy." Vorticism itself, he asserts, is an "intensive art" that leads the poet
to create an image, an "emotional and intellectual complex in
an instant of time." Pound also calls the image "a radiant node
or cluster . . . a Vortex, from which and through which and into

which, ideas are constantly rushing." All experience, he adds,
"rushes into this vortex." Pound's explanation helps us to understand the vortex as containing a still center, a stillness that
is important to Lewis as well. The vortex is centrifugal, but
within its center the force dissipates and leaves a calm. For
Lewis as a painter, the still center that the artist inhabits in his
or her Vortex is the *willed* stillness of a magus in control. Lewis
has written, "We must constantly strive to ENRICH abstraction
till there is almost plain life, or rather to get deeply enough
immersed in material life to experience the shaping power
amongst its vibrations, and to accentuate and perpetuate
these. Here Lewis confirms his commitment to life, or reality, or
nature, but he also suggests that the artist must capture
through the shaping power of art something beyond life—if
not something transcendent, then something "willed," primitive, caught up from something primordial (a Gaudier word),
perhaps something of Pound's "power of the voodoo," or what
Pound described in writing about Epstein's *Doves* (1913) as "the
immutable, the calm thoroughness of unchanging relations,
they are as the gods of the Epicureans, apart, unconcerned,
unrelenting."[19]

When Lewis makes fun of the Cubists with their two apples
and a mandolin, he is objecting to a realism that he calls
"passive," to the Cubists' fondness for static, banal, and traditional objects that are irrelevant to the machine age. Picasso,
the Cubist, on the other hand, is a realist, a materialist. He
gathers up the objects of the world. His abstraction, his
Cubism, is not the asymmetry of an artist aspiring to a force of
"will and consciousness." He captures on his canvas what *is*, to
the point of breaking down the forms of an object in order to
see this object not as a surface in a fixed space but as a form
maneuvering in all its dimensions in a movable space that is
out there. Lewis, on the contrary, wanted in those few Vorticist
years to capture in his work something of those violent forces
in humanity that so soon after the publication of B*last No*. 1 in
1914 would be let loose in a terrible war in which Lewis fought

Edith Sitwell, by Wyndham Lewis (The Tate Gallery, London, Courtesy of Omar S. Pound; © Estate of Mrs. G. A. Wyndham Lewis, by permission)

and that would radically alter his beliefs and change his art from what Reed Way Dasenbrock calls "a dynamic formism" to a more determined figurative art.[20]

The war, Lewis wrote in 1950,

> was a sleep, deep and animal, in which I was visited by images of an order very new to me. Upon waking, I found an altered world; and I had changed, too, very much. The geometrics which had interested me so exclusively before, I now felt were bleak and empty. They wanted filling. They were still as much present to my mind as ever, but submerged in the coloured vegetation, the flesh and blood, that is life.[21]

"The flesh and blood, that is life" were transformed into the portraits of the twenties and thirties. Consider the 1923 portrait of the poet Edith Sitwell, a portrait that illustrates Lewis's finest ability as a painter—his ability to "bury Euclid deep in

the living flesh," to combine "Nature and Design." The geo-
metric treatment lends the figure an impassivity that Timothy
Materer notes in the portrait, and yet there is a psychological
astuteness arising from the quiet, self-assured stance that says
something more about this defiant yet essentially unsuc-
cessful poet.

The 1939 portrait of Pound with its Cubist facial contours,
revealing strong head, imperviously closed eyes, and the poet's
posture of ease and defiance again reveal an artist devoted to a
modernist aesthetics that still has not dispensed with an older
figurative art. The 1938 portrait of T. S. Eliot provoked an uproar
because of its rejection by the Royal Academy, an institution
that Lewis had often attacked for its conservatism. Here Lewis
concentrates on Eliot's intensity and intellect. The body manifests a constriction, with its correct lounge suit and waistcoat
and the hands that are uncomfortably posed. There seems to
be a disjunction, in fact, between the intense preoccupation
exhibited in the face and the uneasy bodily positioning. The
characteristic parting of the hair reinforces this sense of constriction. The shadow of the head on the pale green panel adds
strangeness to the portrait, just as the organic abstract forms
on the sides of the panel contrast with the rather rigid planes of
the poet's face.

The war killed Gaudier-Brzeska—and now he has become a
legend. The Pompidou Center in Paris honors him, and in the
Museum of Modern Art's 1984 show "Primitivism in Twentieth-
Century Art," a Gaudier *Portrait of Ezra Pound* (1914) carved in
wood was shown. His first individual New York show took place
only in 1977 at the Gruenebaum Gallery. I was appalled at this
show, for, except for the exhibition of drawings, it was a disaster.
What would this "Savage Messiah" have thought to see his
original carvings, chiefly in stone, transformed into expensive
casts of bronze—this artist who had carved in the trenches a
Maternity out of the butt of a German rifle, to whom direct
carving was all, and who, according to Richard Aldington, used

Ezra Pound, 1939, by Wyndham Lewis (The Tate Gallery, London, Courtesy of Omar S. Pound; © Estate of Mrs. G. A. Wyndham Lewis, by permission)

to go out late at night with the sculptor Jacob Epstein "and steal pieces of stone from a mason's yard near the Tate Gallery." In their transformations, these bronzes seemed decorative, sculptures for a salon, hardly the work of an artist who had written, "The sculpture I admire is the work of craftsmen. Every inch of the surface is won at the point of the chisel—every stroke of the hammer is a physical and mental effort. No more arbitrary translations of a design in any material."[22]

Ezra Pound's eyes did not deceive him in 1913 when he first saw the work of Henri Gaudier-Brzeska. The sculptor has indeed left his mark on an early British modernism that Wyndham Lewis "blasted" into Britain. But now we are in a postmodern world, nostalgic, antimodern, and anti-avant-garde. The political reasons for such a world Lewis had foreseen. In *Blast No.* 2 he had prophesied that "perpetual war may well be our next

civilization . . . with hosts of spies and endless national con-
fusions . . . |with| miles of wire and steel mazes, and entangle-
ments crackling with electricity." His prophecy has come true. It
is no wonder that the art world has responded with bleak,
passionless "photo pieces" of the contemporary British artists
Gilbert and George or the astonishing harrowing work of the
masterly Francis Bacon, with the Transavantgardists of Italy and
the Neo-Expressionists of Germany and America.

Perhaps Pound was right when he said in 1963, "The modern
world doesn't exist because nothing exists which does not
understand its past or its future. The world of today exists only
as a fusion, a span in time."[23]

4

Pound's Economics

James Laughlin

Time was when we could read *The Cantos* without worrying too much about Pound's economic theories. We could put them down to eccentricity. We could admire the splendor of the Usura canto, the glorious language and the power of the rhythm, but skip over the monetary history in Cantos 96 and 97. We had to know something about the economics to understand the sorrows and, in his own word, the "errors" which he acknowledged in his last years. But we did not grasp, or at least I did not grasp, many of the implications of the ideas about money in the texture of the poem.

Such separation is no longer possible, because of an astonishing paper, "Ezra Pound: The Economy of Poetry/The Poetry of Economics," forthcoming by Richard Sieburth of New York University. After this paper, which applies semiotic, psychoanalytic, and Marxist methods of criticism to Pound's conceptions of monetary and poetic representation, we will never again be able to read *The Cantos* without seeing linguistic connections which we did not recognize before. Sieburth's analysis of the relationship between Pound's writings and his economic theories is so complex that I cannot possibly give a fair summary of it. But some of the main themes turn on poetry and naming and the minting of money. Sieburth deals with Pound's obsession with the stamp of sovereignty impressed on money and equally on poetry. He points out a pervasive duality, or "doubling." Usury is thus the excremental doppelgänger of poetic gold. Sieburth compares the "doubling" of poetry and economics in Pound's work to Freud's interpretation of the antithetical meaning of some primary words. *Sacred* usually means "holy" but can also mean "defiled"; *altus* is both "high" and "low." Sieburth "deconstructs" these reversibilities in Pound's work until we are almost ready to believe that his surname (£) predestined him to become a poet-economist and that "Ezry/Usury" is more than a pun.

In his later years, as he moved toward silence, Pound wrote me of his worry that he could not make *The Cantos* "cohere." Sieburth suggests that Pound believed he could write the poem on credit ("the future tense of money"), a loan which would be repaid in full when the "paradise" cantos eventually made the whole structure clear. But to our sorrow, Pound's declining health did not permit the triumphant and revelatory closure. The last drafts and fragments are beautiful, but they are subdued and often melancholy. Canto 120, however, with which the book now ends, is not the correct ending. The preferred ending is the preceding fragment on page 802.[1] It, too, is subdued but ends with the sturdy imperative: "To be men not destroyers." In this spirit Pound gave battle to the bankers—a better closure, for the poem and for the life.

People often ask why Pound, whose education was in languages, literature, and history, thought he could become an economist. Quite simply, he identified with Odysseus and knew that he, Ezra Pound, was also polumētis, "a man of cunning and many skills." He could do anything. He made his own furniture and taught himself Chinese from dictionaries. He was slightly tone deaf and could play with only one finger on the clavichord he got from Arnold Dolmetsch, but he wrote two short operas which are still performed. He became a music critic for the New Age almost overnight (as "William Atheling") and soon added art criticism (as "B. H. Diaz"). He failed only as a sculptor. Brancusi gave him some small pieces of stone to cut, but he chucked them in the *poubelle.*

I think we should dispose immediately of the myth that Pound became interested in monetary reform because his grandfather, Thaddeus Coleman Pound, not long after the Civil War printed his own money for the use of the employees of his Union Lumbering Company in Chippewa Falls, Wisconsin. Pound venerated Thaddeus even more than he did the Loomis brothers on his mother's side, who he told me were hanged for stealing horses (though there is no documentation on the hangings), but he admitted that he did not realize the full importance of Thaddeus's scrip until he had studied Silvio Gesell. (One can read about Thaddeus, who appears as Thaddeus Cuthbertson Weight, in Pound's *Indiscretions,* which can now be found most easily in the collection called *Pavannes & Divagations.*)[2]

Another explanation, which probably has more substance, is that there is a direct line of causation between the death of Pound's great friend the sculptor Henri Gaudier-Brzeska in the First World War and Pound's getting into credit reform. This proposition, and one hears it often, is that Pound was rocked by Gaudier's death and so many others.

> There died a myriad,
> And of the best among them,
> For an old bitch gone in the teeth,
> For a botched civilization.

And a bit earlier in *Mauberley* he wrote:

> Died some, pro patria,
>   non "dulce" non "et decor" . . .

walked eye-deep in hell
believing in old men's lies, then unbelieving
came home, home to a lie,
home to many deceits,
home to old lies and new infamy;
usury age-old and age-thick.

Pound then set out to study the causes of war, concluding that armament makers and bankers were as much responsible as generals and politicians. Schneider-Creusot, he discovered, sold cannons to both France and Germany. Looking into banking, he learned that banks created money for loans "ex nihil," simply by book entry, listing loans as a form of deposits. (The permitted ratio of "loan deposits" to real deposits varies, but in this country today it can go as high as nine to one.)

Said Paterson:
Hath benefit of interest on all
the moneys which it, the bank, creates out of nothing
(46/233)

So Pound was more than ripe for Social Credit when he met C. H. Douglas in A. R. Orage's office at the *New Age* in 1918. But from my conversations with him, I suspect that the Gaudier-Douglas chain was only a part of Pound's motivation. Consider his poverty during the years in London. He was the hot young poet around town but so poor that he often had to write to his father in Wyncote, "Dear Dad, Can you send me five dollars?" (There are a number of such appeals in the collection of letters to his parents which Mary de Rachewiltz is now editing.) Along with that penury was his confidence that he was on the way to becoming a great poet. Not surprisingly, he was convinced that the economic system should be so ordered as to provide a living for writers and artists. It did not do so because the banks controlled the system, making money scarce so that they might lend it at high rates. Canto 45 centers chiefly on artists. But certainly the plight of poets was in his mind long before that canto was written.

Much later, one of the attractions of Mussolini may have been that Pound fantasized that Mussolini could be educated to crack down on the Italian banks and that Il Duce might reincarnate as Sigismondo Malatesta, who was not only a doughty warrior but a patron of artists and scholars, setting up grants for writers. Alas, as far as I can determine, the only Italian writer who got a stipend was Pirandello, a longtime Fascist.

When we speak of Pound's economics, we think of him first as a Social Creditor. His economics began with Social Credit but went far beyond this movement. I cannot prove it, but Pound may have been the inventor, intellectually at least, of the Cuisinart. He kept pouring new ingredients into the ever-protesting gullet of Major Douglas. I am not certain of the exact dates of the contaminations, but there followed Gesellism, with its stamp scrip and velocity of circulation; the attacks on usury by the canonists such as Saint Ambrose; his research into the history of the Monte dei Paschi bank in Siena; the history of coinage in the books of Alexander Del Mar; the structure of the Fascist corporations; the cullings from Jefferson, Adams, and Van Buren; the ideas of Confucius and Mencius on taxation; and borrowings from many contemporary writers—Brooks Adams, Montgomery Butchart, Irving Fisher, Christopher Hollis, Arthur Kitson, P. J. Larranaga, A. R. Orage, Willis Overholser, Odon Por, Frederick Soddy, Jerry Voorhis, McNair Wilson, W. E. Woodward, and others. (See the Appendix at the end of this chapter.) He even found a clue in a Latin translation of Aristotle: *Nummum nummus non parit,* "money does not beget money," a phrase that does not seem to have found its way into *The Cantos*, probably because he would have had to revise it to *nummum nummus parire non debet*, "money *should* not beget money."

By the time of the Second World War, Pound's articles had

become so heretical, such a potpourri, that the high-church Douglasite magazines would no longer print them. He began sending them to me to have them printed in this country, but I did not have much luck. For some strange reason *Harper's* and the *Atlantic* were not enthusiastic. And in a letter of 1937, we find Pound asking H. L. Mencken, "Who the hell cares about Doug. schemes?" By then the disenchantment had become mutual.

Clifford Hugh Douglas, the inventor of Social Credit, died in 1952 at the age of 73. He was a successful British engineer who worked for Westinghouse in India, for a railroad in Argentina, and for the London Post Office tube system. At some point he must have been in the army; he was always called "Major." Douglas's first book, *Economic Democracy*, which Orage helped him write, was serialized in the *New Age* in 1919. He went on to write nine more books, developing his themes and their implications for a better society. He was an ardent believer in democracy and no socialist. (Pound used to tell me that "Marx never understood money.") The fact that Douglas was able to get so many books published shows that his movement had considerable support in England, as well as in New Zealand and in the Canadian province of Alberta. (The American Social Credit party, of which I was a member while at Harvard, never got very far, despite the handbills which I distributed in the cars of the Boston Mass Transit and despite the excellent magazine *New Democracy*, which the critic Gorham Munson edited in New York.)

Douglas was not trained as an economist, but with an engineer's savvy for what made things work—and not work—he detected flaws in the world's economic system. He observed that in wartime there was an abundance of credit for armaments but that in peacetime there was a shortage of credit for social uses, for expanding business and employment. Douglas's books are not nearly so dry as most textbooks of economics, but they are hardly entertaining, and now, with the increasing complexity of our system, they are not up to date.

However, I have made a fairly complete bibliography, along with lists of some of Pound's writings on economics and of the books by others which influenced him. (See the Appendix.)

Prophets are not necessarily their own best explainers. E. S. Holter did a primer called *Social Credit* (1934), but the most useful book is Gorham Munson's *Aladdin's Lamp* (1945), which covers the whole area of credit reform. Hugh Kenner, of course, has a stimulating chapter on Douglas in *The Pound Era*. And Earl Davis's book *Vision Fugitive: Ezra Pound and Economics* (1968) is a comprehensive introduction.

As we look at Social Credit, I consider Douglas and Orage a team. Not only did Orage coach Douglas with his writing, and probably often rewrote him, he was the social philosopher of the doctrine. As Wendy Flory points out, "Orage supplied the visionary quality to the statistical basis of Social Credit." Orage's vision of "a more humane society" (which we must compare with Pound's dream of a *paradiso terrestre*) gave Social Credit much of its appeal. As Pound wrote in the ABC *of Economics*, "Economics, as science, has no messianic call to alter the instincts." But a call was needed to get action.

The central position of Social Credit was Douglas's controversial contention that total costs exceed total purchasing power. (It is said that this revelation came to him when he was going over the accounts of the Royal Aircraft Works at Farnborough.) Douglas expressed this shortfall in his A + B theorem. A stands for income—principally salaries, wages, and dividends, which enter the economy as purchasing power. B represents plant and bank costs, which, Douglas claimed, do not contribute to purchasing power. A will not purchase B, he said. No "reputable," orthodox economist has ever been known to endorse the A + B theorem. It is seen as an oversimplification because it does not take into account the timing and rates of flow of money movements. Pound, of course, dismissed these objections as part of the stupidity of the academics in the despised "beaneries," who were all under the thumb of the

banks to keep their jobs. And he explained to me that Thread-
needle Street (the Bank of England) had ordered Fleet Street
(the London press) never to print Douglas's name, even to the
point that, when Douglas was invited to the queen's garden
party at Buckingham Palace, his name was missing from the
guest list.

Douglas's proposal for increasing purchasing power to meet
the A + B shortfall was the National Dividend, an interesting
variant on Keynes and perhaps an early form of monetarism.
All citizens, except those whose income was four times the
amount of the dividend, would go to the post office to collect
their dividend, for which they needed to do no work because
they were entitled to it as children of the sun. That rationale, at
least, was provided me by John Hargrave, the leader of the
British Social Credit party. The amount of the dividend would
fluctuate periodically, being calibrated to the rates of production and consumption. A national monetary authority would
do the computations. These infusions would raise purchasing
power above costs and so increase employment.

Orage and Douglas shrewdly foresaw that technology and
robotics would reduce jobs. They conceived that the time would
come when there could not be full employment and the National Dividend would sustain those who had no work. Today
welfare and unemployment insurance furnish this protection,
at great cost to the taxpayer. The source of funds for the dividends would be the same as now used for monetary expansion—book entry, but on the books of the state, not the banks.
There would be no interest for the banks and no burden on the
taxpayer. It would be *social* credit, based on the productive capacity of the nation and the ability of its people to exploit their
skills and "the abundance of nature." What is this flimflam of
just more printing-press money? To understand, we must try to
put ourselves in the minds of the Social Creditors and forget all
traditional principles of economics. Social Credit rejects gold
and the idea that money is a limited commodity. Pound always

said that money was simply a ticket to get goods and services from one place to another. The purpose of money was to distribute abundance to everyone. You don't need kilometers, he said, to build a road.

The idea of a National Dividend understandably provoked indignation. The poor protested that, despite the exclusions, the middle classes had no right to it, and the rich complained that the lower classes were mostly shiftless and had enough dole already. Less prejudiced individuals suggested that so much new money would lead to inflation. Douglas's answer was a mechanism he called the "Just Price," a retail discount which would peg selling prices to the real cost of production, exclusive of *financial* costs. Like the dividend, the discount would fluctuate to achieve the right balance between inflation and deflation. It represents price controls, such as many nations have used in wartime. Pound's belief in the Just Price was confirmed by his turning up a similar concept in his study of some of the canonists in Migne, though with them, I think, the concern was more with Christian morality than with turning the economic wheels.

To me the appeal of the National Dividend is that it would inject new money—and new money is apparently necessary for an expanding economy—throughout the social pyramid so that it would work its way up to those at the top (who, as we all know, most deserve it) but in the process give much comfort to those less smart or industrious. As things are now—if I understand the system correctly—an increase in the money supply is ordained by the Federal Reserve but is put out through the banks, who use a fair part of it to finance such questionable causes as the takeover of one huge corporation by another, loans to Latin America which will never be repaid, or "Star Wars" factories—but who do not loan much money to needy residents of Newark or Bedford Stuyvesant.

Silvio Gesell was not a famous economist, but Pound tells us in Canto 74 that he was minister of finance for "rather less than five days" in the Lindhauer socialist government of Bavaria following the First World War. Gesell was a German who had made a fortune in Argentina and began to think about the nature and flow of money. Gesell's invention was *Schwundgeld*, or stamp scrip, a self-liquidating currency which would discourage hoarding and increase the velocity of circulation. This Wörgl money was a measure of work. The legend on my ten-schilling note from Wörgl in Austria is interesting. It reads, *Nothilfe Wörgl Bestätigter Arbeitswerk,"* "Wörgl help in emergency, confirmed value of work."

Schwund means "dwindling." *Schwundgeld*, mechanically, was a bill with squares on the back on which the bearer must periodically place a postage stamp to keep it valid. A fully stamped note would be replaced at the bank by a new one. Details of the system appear in Gesell's book *The New Economic Order.* It is subtitled "A plan to secure an uninterrupted exchange of the products of labor, free from bureaucratic interference, usury, and exploitation."

Stamp scrip, as Pound pointed out, put a tax on money itself, but one that would be paid by those who could afford it. Is there some comparison with Henry George's "single tax," which was to tax only land, not income? Like Confucius and Mencius, Pound disapproved of unfair taxation, which was probably the primary basis for his supporting Gesell's theory. Gesell also opposed unearned income such as interest and rents. (See pages 205, 441–42, and 507 in *The Cantos* for references to Gesell.)

Gesell's *Schwundgeld* was apparently implemented on a strictly local basis only, in the communities of Wörgl and Schwanenkirchen in Austria. One of my most interesting trips with Ezra and Olga was driving them from Venice up to Gais to see Mary and then over the Brenner to visit Herr Unterguggenberger, the deposed mayor of Wörgl. Wörgl is a pleasant town of about six thousand on the River Inn in the mountains of the

Tyrol. It is usually rather prosperous, being a junction point on the railroad between Munich, the Brenner, and Vienna, with lumbering from the mountains and good farms in the valley bottoms. But the depression hit it hard, and no money was circulating. Unterguggenberger had heard of *Schwundgeld* and printed some for the town. Pound tells about the Wörgl experiment on page 314 of the *Selected Prose*, how *Schwundgeld* was restoring prosperity for three years until "all the lice of Europe, Rothschildian and otherwise," found out about it and had the central bank in Vienna crack down on it. Or as he presents it in Canto 74:

> the state need not borrow
> as was shown by the mayor of Wörgl
> who had a milk route
> and whose wife sold shirts and short breeches
> and on whose book-shelf was the Life of Henry Ford
> and also a copy of the Divina Commedia
> and of the Gedichte of Heine
> a nice little town in the Tyrol in a wide flat-lying valley
> near Innsbruck and when a note of the
> small town of Wörgl went over
> a counter in Innsbruck
> and the banker saw it go over
> all the slobs in Europe were terrified
> "no one" said the Frau Burgomeister
> "in this village who cd/ write a newspaper article.
> Knew it was money but pretended it was not
> in order to be on the safe side of the law."
>
> (74/441)

I know how much Gesellism meant to Pound from a letter he wrote me in 1970, one of the last letters I had from him, in which he still worried about stamp scrip. He said, "Stamp scrip is impractical as, even when the bills were printed on really good paper, they wore out and went back to treasury to be pulped at end of six months. Also the bother of looking at each separate note to see if it was properly stamped. This does not exclude the use of local money in an emergency."

Alexander Del Mar was another of Pound's great enthusiasms. Periodically he urged me to reprint one of Del Mar's books, but I never got interested. Del Mar (1836–1926), like Douglas, was an engineer, though chiefly in mining. His avocations were the study of precious metals, the history of coinage, and monetary systems. He published some thirty books with such titles as *Money and Civilization* and *Roman and Moslem Moneys*. But the one which appealed most to Pound was Del Mar's *History of Monetary Crimes*, which explored the sovereignty of money and how good rulers throughout history had controlled, and bad ones had manipulated, first coinage and later currency and credit. Del Mar believed that a high civilization required an exclusive system of money issued and guaranteed by the state. This view ties in with Pound's repeated insistence that the Constitution gave Congress the sole right to issue money (see art. 1, sec. 8: "The Congress shall have power . . . to coin money, regulate the value thereof, and of foreign coin, and fix the standard of weights and measures"), a right which was taken over by banks, a capture which the resistance of Adams, Jefferson, Jackson, Van Buren, and Lincoln could not reverse. There are sprinklings from Del Mar's books on coinage in Cantos 89, 96, and 97.

Usury, of course, is a major element in Pound's economics. Douglas and Orage, however, did not often use the word in Ezra's sense of it, but were more likely to speak of "bank charges." Pound's sense of usury came, I think, from the canonist writers, principally Saint Ambrose. At the end of the great Canto 45, Pound defined usury:

> N. B. Usury: A charge for the use of purchasing power, levied without regard to production; often without regard to the possibilities of production. (Hence the failure of the Medici bank.)

This position is Social Credit doctrine, of course, but in Pound's mind it was tied to Saint Ambrose and to the Monte dei Paschi bank of Siena. The linking phrase is Ambrose's *captans anonam maledictus in plebe sit*, which Professor Wilhelm has located in Ambrose's *De Tobia* (*Patrologia latina*, vol. 14), a commentary on the apocryphal Book of Tobias. Pound translated *captans anonam* as "hoggers of the harvest." The *De Tobia* attacked Jewish usurers who ruined farmers with high rates of interest on crop loans. (Duke Leopold of Siena was one of Pound's heroes because he limited the Monte dei Paschi to 3 percent on loans to the peasants.) Pound had nothing against bank loans which support any kind of production at a fair rate. And he had nothing against service banking. In fact, all his life he had a savings account at a bank in Jenkintown, Pennsylvania.

Some Poundians foolishly sweep Pound's anti-Semitism under the rug, although there is ample documentation of it, especially in the Rome broadcasts. We must face it. But something which Dr. Winfred Overholser, the chief psychiatrist at St. Elizabeths, told me has always helped me to live with it. Overholser said that Pound's anti-Semitism must be judged medically, not morally. He diagnosed it as a common aspect of paranoia—the need for a scapegoat. Pound's paranoia came from insufficient acclaim for *The Cantos*, no acceptance of his economic theories, and his inability to make a decent living as a writer. The Usura canto focuses on what usury does to artists, but the same applies to poets.

> Usura rusteth the chisel
> It rusteth the craft and the craftsman.
> (45/230)

When I was at the "Ezuversity" in 1934–35 the anti-Semitism showed only in jokes. But when Pound came to the United States in 1939, it was increasing. (If only the Swedes had given him the Nobel Prize, everything might have been different!)

Fascism was part of Pound's economics because of the corporations, which were rather like guilds and were Mussolini's replacement for labor unions. The corporations, Pound told me, would make an ideal social basis for the implementation of Social Credit. Although Pound was working on his *Jefferson and/or Mussolini* in 1934, he did not give me much detail about the corporations. The book is extremely discursive, but it does have a central theme: the Jeffersonian political tradition had been reborn, not in Virginia, but in Mussolini's Italy.

Should we take Pound's economic theories seriously? Certainly we must be aware of them to understand *The Cantos* and his life. But do they have any practical application for the muddle we are in today? I think that Pound had cracker-barrel horse sense about the pyramiding of debt, both public and private. And I think Douglas and Orage were right in trying to make credit rather than debt the basis of the economy. I grant that much government interest provides income that is spent. Yet much of the national debt is held by banks.

Private debt is astronomical. Again, dividends and interest contribute to spendable income. But what about the takeovers among giant industries? DuPont eats Conoco. SoCal swallows Gulf. The acquiring companies accomplish these engorgements through loans given by banks at high interest. Then for decades the acquiring companies will use their profits to pay back the loans and the interest. Mergers do not reduce unemployment, and stockholders suffer. A dozen investment banking firms are scouting these deals for industrial companies. This system is bank capitalism at its worst. Is this the right way to use credit—which is fundamentally based on the people's faith in the government—for productive purposes?

The book *Funny Money*, by Marc Singer (New York: Knopf, 1985) would have delighted Pound. It documents how some young bankers in Oklahoma City used Paterson's principle of creating book-entry money to make high-interest loans to gas drillers. The bankers' little Penn Square Bank nearly bankrupted the great Continental Bank of Illinois. I understand that to date Washington has had to pour nearly seven billion dollars of the taxpayer's money into saving Continental Illinois to prevent a domino-effect collapse of other major money-center banks.

Many banking practices beyond the creation of money "ex nihil" are concealed from the public. But one surfaced in the *New York Times* business section on June 24, 1985, under the heading "Worrisome Bank Obligations." Federal bank regulators apparently do not require banks to include on their balance sheets loan guarantees or commitments to make loans, though they collect fees on them. The *Times* reporter estimated the value of these hidden instruments at over a trillion dollars. Paterson never did that well. And most people are unaware, as Alfred Kazin points out in chapter 2, of the present campaign by the banks to tamper with state usury regulations so that they may raise their rates on credit-card interest.

Pound's wit makes the style of many of his economic writings diverting, but one sequence is really comical—the verses which he did for the *New English Weekly* as Alfie Venison, the Poet of Titchfield Street. These poems are reprinted as Appendix 2 of *Personae* and include the following:

> "Song of Six Hundred M.P's"
> We are 'ere met together
>   in this momentous hower,
> Ter lick th' bankers' dirty boots
>   an keep the Bank in power.
> We are 'ere met together
>   ter grind the same old axes
> And keep the people in its place
>   a'payin' us the taxes.

> We are six hundred beefy men
> (but mostly gas and suet)
> An' every year we meet to let
> some other feller do it.

Pound's economic theories were a mishmash of eccentricities. But they were inspired by his millennial optimism and his assurance that he knew the answers. He wanted to create the paradiso terrestre of a just economic system without resorting to socialism or revolution. *The Cantos* themselves, with their revisions of history and their citation of honest men of the past—Adams and Jefferson, certain Chinese emperors, Duke Leopold, and others—were part of the process. (In Canto 71, Adams tells us that "every bank of discount is downright corruption.") But Pound's dream may never come true except in his own imaginary cities, such as Wagadu, which he constructed from one of Frobenius's African legends:

> 4 times was the city rebuilded . . .
> now in the mind indestructible . . .
> With the four giants at the four corners.
>   (74/430)

And Dioce, which he found in Herodotus, "to build the city of Dioce whose terraces are the colour of stars" (74/425). In Herodotus the city of Deioces had its battlements plated with silver and gold. Why did Pound turn silver and gold into the "colour of stars"? Was it because "colour of stars" is so beautiful, as image and as language, or because, without realizing it, he did not wish to signify the sovereignty of money in his sacred city?

A Selective Bibliography
on Pound's Economic Ideas

Books by Ezra Pound

ABC *of Economics*. London: Faber and Faber, 1933. This work should be
the basic text, but it is written in a boring way—simplistic, re-

petitive, and at times overelaborated. Pound set out to write a
primer and abandoned all his usual vitalities of personal style.
Most of the short pieces on economic themes in part 6 of his
Selected Prose (see below) are more lively and instructive on specific
points. See, for example, "A Study of Relations and Gesell,"
pp. 272–82.

"Ezra Pound Speaking": Radio Speeches of World War II. Edited by Leonard
W. Doob. Westport, Conn.: Greenwood Press, 1978.

Guide to Kulchur. New York: New Directions, 1952. The *Guide* contains
scattered discussions of economic themes.

Impact. Edited by Noel Stock. Chicago: Regnery, 1960. Except the brief
article "Destruction by Taxation," most of the economic pieces in
this collection are in *Selected Prose*.

The Money Pamphlets Series. In 1950 or 1951, Pound edited a series of
pamphlets on economic subjects which were published by his
disciple Peter Russell in London, using Pound's own texts. This
entire series appears in *Selected Prose*.

The Selected Letters of Ezra Pound. Edited by D. D. Paige. London: Faber
and Faber, 1971. The letters in this volume end at 1930 and occasionally include comments on economic themes.

Selected Prose, 1909–1965. Edited by William Cookson. London: Faber
and Faber, 1973. Part 6, "Civilization, Money, and History," contains
twenty-six important pieces, many of which deal at least mar-
ginally with economics (e.g., "ABC of Economics," "An Introduction
to the Economic Nature of the United States," "Gold and Work,
1944," "Banks," "A Visiting Card," and "What Is Money For?").

Source Books Which Pound Used in Developing
His Economic Theories

Adams, Brooks. *The Law of Civilization and Decay*. New York: Macmillan,
1897.

Benton, Thomas Hart. *Thirty Years' View*. 1854. 2d ed. New York: Ap-
pleton, 1856.

Butchart, Montgomery. *Money*. London: S. Nott, 1935.

Del Mar, Alexander. *Ancient Britain Revisited*. New York: Cambridge Encyclopedia, 1889.

––––––. *A History of Monetary Crimes*. Moscow, Idaho: Clearwater Pub-
lishers, n.d.

————. *History of Monetary Systems*. 1895. Reprint. Orono, Maine: National Poetry Foundation, 1983.

————. *A History of Money in America*. New York: Cambridge Encyclopedia, 1889.

————. *The Middle Ages Revisited*. New York: Cambridge Encyclopedia, 1900.

————. *Money and Civilization*. London: G. Bell and Sons, 1886.

————. *Roman and Moslem Moneys*. Washington, D.C.: Square Dollar Series, 1955.

————. *The Science of Money*. London: G. Bell and Sons, 1885.

Douglas, C. H. *The Alberta Experiment*. London: Eyre and Spottiswoode, 1937.

————. *The Control and Distribution of Production*. London: C. Palmer, 1922.

————. *Credit-Power and Democracy*. London: C. Palmer, 1920.

————. *The Douglas Manual*. Edited by Philip Mairet. Toronto: C. M. Dent and Sons, 1934.

————. *Economic Democracy*. London: C. Palmer, 1920.

————. *The Monopoly of Credit*. London: Chapman and Hall, 1931.

————. *The Nature of Democracy*. London: S. Nott, 1934.

————. *Social Credit*. London: C. Palmer, 1924.

————. *The Use of Money*. New York: New Economics Group, 1934.

————. *Warning Democracy*. London: C. M. Grieve, 1931.

Fisher, Irving. *Stabilized Money*. London: Allen and Unwin, 1935.

Gesell, Silvio. *The Natural Economic Order*. Translated by Philip Pye. 2 vols. San Antonio, Tex.: Free Economy Publishing, 1934–36.

Hollis, Christopher. *The Two Nations*. London: G. Routledge and Sons, 1935.

Kitson, Arthur. *A Scientific Solution to the Money Question*. Boston: Arena Publishing, 1895.

Larranaga, P. J. *Gold, Glut, and Government*. London: Allen and Unwin, 1932.

Orage, A. R. *An Alphabet of Economics*. London: T. F. Unwin, 1917.

Overholser, Willis A. *A History of Money in the United States*. Libertyville, Ill.: Progress Publishing Concern, 1936.

Por, Odon. *Italy's Policy of Social Economics, 1930–40*. Translated by Ezra Pound. Bergamo, Italy: Istituto italiano d'arti grafiche, 1941.

Soddy, Frederick. *The Role of Money*. London: G. Routledge and Sons, 1934.

————. *Wealth, Virtual Wealth, and Debt*. 2d ed. New York: Dutton, 1933.
Van Buren, Martin. *The Autobiography of Martin Van Buren*. Edited by John
    C. Fitzpatrick. Washington, D.C.: Government Printing Office, 1920.
Voorhis, Jerry. *Out of Debt, Out of Danger*. New York: Devin-Adair, 1943.
Wilson, Robert McNair. *The Mind of Napoleon: A Study of Napoleon, Mr.
    Roosevelt, and the Money Power*. London: G. Routledge and Sons, 1934.
Woodward, W. E. *A New American History*. New York: Farrar and
    Rinehart, 1936.

Books about Pound's Economics and Related Subjects

Davis, Earle. *Vision Fugitive*. Lawrence: University Press of Kansas,
    1968.
Hargrave, John. *Social Credit Clearly Explained*. London: SCP Publishing
    House, 1945.
Holter, Elizabeth Sage. *Social Credit*. London: S. Nott, 1934.
Kenner, Hugh. *The Pound Era*. Berkeley and Los Angeles: University of
    California Press, 1971.
Munson, Gorham. *Aladdin's Lamp*. New York: Creative Age Press, 1945.

5

Pound's Cantos and Confucianism

Chang Yao-hsin

When Ezra Pound appeared on the scene in the first years of the present century, the West presented a panorama of wasteland. T. S. Eliot saw around him nothing but "Rocks, moss, stone-crop, iron, merds" and "A heap of broken images, where the sun beats, / And the dead tree gives no shelter." It was a world, as Warren French describes it, "littered with the dead fragments of dead civilizations and the fading hopes of dying religions," a world in which, as Yeats puts it, "The best lack all conviction, while the worst / Are full of passionate intensity." In the same way, Pound saw pervasive and impenetrable gloom everywhere and felt no desire to flatter America by pretending that "we are at present enduring anything except the Dark Ages." He saw barbarism rampant in a beastly and cantankerous age, but no organized or coordinated civilization. To him the world is all chaos and disorder; life is a sordid and personally crushing oppression, and culture produces nothing but all sorts of "intangible bondage." It is only natural that he began his career with a grand abnegation. "The principal subject of *The Cantos* as a whole poem, the only one capable of subsuming the subjects of the individual cantos and of drawing them all into one intelligible system of meanings," says W. M. Frohock, "is the objection to life as it is now lived, not merely its politics and its economics, but also its art, its religion, and its metaphysics."[1]

Pound saw no effective cure in Christianity for the disease of his times. He could have agreed with Joseph Wood Krutch, who saw humanity's helplessness in a hostile society. He could have agreed with Bertrand Russell, who did not believe in a beneficent God. In the faithless Western world, the Christian God seemed to be replaced by a God created by people's love of the good. In his grand abnegation, Pound turned his back on Christianity. Official Christianity was a "sink." "I refuse to accept ANY monotheistic taboos whatsoever," he said in a letter of 1922; "I consider . . . the Hebrew scriptures the record of a barbarian tribe, full of evil." "I don't mind the Christian religion," he said in another context; "organized religions have nearly always done more harm than good, and they have always constituted a danger." With time his attack on Christianity and the Holy Scripture became increasingly ferocious. In a letter in 1940, he called the Bible "poison" that had been for centuries instilled into helpless babes and dumped on adults like god-blithering tosh, low moral tone, black superstition, and general filth. He regarded the whole thing as a perversion, a poor substitute for truth. He repeated approvingly the comment of Young Tching (Yung Cheng, a Manchu emperor), who said that "Christians are such sliders and liars" (61/334).[2] Pound's railing at all religions in the filthiest possible language in his *Cantos* ("shit and religion always stinking in concord" [56/306]) was certainly no positive reflection on Christianity.

As time went on he even lost faith in the value of Greek literature and philosophy. "The Greek philosophers have been served up as highbrows," he said in *Guide to Kulchur.* "We know them as ideas, each handed us as a maxim." Greek thought is, he felt, utterly irresponsible; at no point is it impregnated with

a feeling for the whole people. Dante was great, and so was
Sophocles, but they came after Confucius. Aristotle may have
been great, too, but he was not fit even to clean the boots of
Confucius. "Aristotle's hedging, backing and filling, if you compare it with a true work like the Ta Hio ('The Great Learning'), is a
give away. This bloke, were he alive today, wd. be writing crap for
the 'Utilities!' He has lasted because 'like to like.' He is not a
man with the truth in him."[3]

With the two major elements on which Western tradition
reposes thus ruthlessly written off, virtually nothing remained
but a spiritual and intellectual vacuum. "Worship the god created by our own love of the good," the voice of Bertrand Russell
boomed. Pound, when he looked about and turned East, found
a messiah in Confucius, who enunciated "the principle of the
good" and the medicine for the disease of the West in his Ta Hio.
As the one lantern under the cabin roof (49/244), Confucius,
Pound believed, could enlighten and civilize the barbarous
Occident.[4] The wisdom of the Confucian classic Ta Hio was, as
Pound saw it, not yet exhausted and indeed inexhaustible. As
contained in the forty-six characters of the "Text of Confucius,"
which opens "The Great Learning," that wisdom boils down in
the final analysis to one notion: order and tranquility, from
which light shines forth. Order and tranquility come from enlightened rule, and two salient features of Confucian enlightened rule are equitable distribution of wealth and light
taxation. These ideals constitute the thematic concerns of the
Chinese cantos (Cantos 13, 49, 52–61) and in a sense underlie
The Cantos as a whole. Canto 13 underscores the idea of order;
Canto 49 engenders a feeling of tranquility; and the eclectic
encapsulation of Chinese history in Cantos 52–61 reveals
Pound's admiration for what he considered to be enlightened
rulers and their enlightened rule. I review first, however,
Pound's cheerless and somber picture of the West.

The world of The Cantos is indeed cheerless and somber.
Canto 1 considers the joyless Hades, where "the cadaverous

dead,"'"the impotent dead," and "the sunless dead" are the only residents. Canto 3 contains the tragic sight of the Spanish hero Ruy Díaz being ostracized and breaking his way to Valencia and also the murder in a decayed Renaissance mansion, the site of "drear waste":

> Ignez da Castra murdered, and a wall
> Here stripped, here made to stand.
> Drear waste, the pigment flakes from the stone,
> Or plaster flakes, Mantegna painted the wall.
> Silk tatters, "Nec Spe Nec Metu."
>
>   (3/12)

Cantos 4 and 5 offer not a ray of sunlight but an expanse of unfruitful world, where the vinestocks lie untended and the north wind nips on the bough and "seas in heart / Toss up chill crests" (5/18). Canto 7 portrays a contemporary society, be it London or Paris, as a world of phantoms and ghosts, one not unlike the world of *Hugh Selwyn Mauberley* and *The Waste Land*:

> And all that day, another day:
>   Thin husks I had known as men.
> Dry casques of departed locusts
>   speaking a shell of speech. . . .
> Propped between chairs and table. . . .
> Words like the locust-shells, moved by no inner being;
>   A dryness calling for death.
>
>   (7/26)

In this world "the dead Lorenzaccio" has more life than the moving husks who live a life of death ("Bend to the tawdry table, / Lift up their spoons to mouths, put forks in cut-lets, / And make sound like the sound of voices" [7/27]), and the poet keenly feels the horror at "the tall indifference [that] moves," and at "the mere living shell." London and Paris become places of locust shells. Skipping over Canto 8, which begins with an ominous quotation from Eliot's epochal work, we come in Canto 11 to witness the rise and fall of the fortunes of the eventually despoiled Malatesta and arrive at a scene (Cantos 14–15) in which there is nothing but perversion and "darkness unconscious" on all conceivable levels of life. Here is hell itself, with all its scatological details, its stench and hell rot, its politicians addressing crowds through their arse holes, its profiteers drinking blood sweetened with shit, and its perverters of language lying for hire—the cesspool of the universe and the bog of stupidities. Most important of all, there is the beast with a hundred legs, "usura," which blasts light, life, and love out of existence. Even in Canto 16, which offers a glimpse of the earthly paradise, we see a Europe very much ruined and destroyed. It is just possible that, had Pound kept strictly to his own province as a poet and resisted the temptation of treating a subject on the whole alien to him, a concern of his which in time amounted to an obsession, he would have enjoyed with Eliot the undisputed honor of initiating modern American poetry. As it was, he stumbled into the quagmire of economics, from which he never managed to extricate himself. Whatever he may have meant, the venture led him to the espousal of a faith which Mussolini shared.

A major thematic concern of The Cantos is the treatment of usury, which takes up an enormous amount of space. Canto 12 talks of banks not likely to ease distribution. Canto 30 mentions how money debases the arts and customs of Venice. Canto 34 records the fact of banks' breaking all over America and prostrating every principle of economy. Canto 37 registers the pernicious effect of the Bank of the United States deranging the country's credit and controlling the public mind. Before the denunciation of the malpractice of the Bank of England in Canto 46, Pound lashed himself into fury at usura in Canto 45 and repeated his charge against both usury and the Jewish people in Canto 51. In short, to Pound, much of the Western disease is derivable from usury and ink money. Hugh Kenner is right when he says that the first fifty cantos paint for us a picture of "the complete and utter inferno of the past century," and so is Angela Jung, who sees these cantos as a vehement condemnation of the cardinal crime against humanity.[5]

A sunny spot in the ambient gloom, Canto 13 shines with the light of Confucius. Here Confucianism undergoes a rigorous process of "telegraphic abbreviation," so much so that, to those who know little about and share none of his faith in Confucianism, Pound is indeed offering platitudes for profound verities.[6] But he manages to keep the quintessence of Confucianism intact. The canto begins with a lyric representation of Confucius, chatting at leisure with his disciples, which is a way of presenting Confucius's ideal of harmony. After a few lines revealing the Chinese philosopher's dedication to society, the canto elucidates the one crucial belief in Confucianism:

> And Kung [Confucius] said, and wrote on the bo leaves:
>> If a man have not order within him
> He can not spread order about him;
> And if a man have not order within him
> His family will not act with due order;
>> And if the prince have not order within him
> He can not put order in his dominions.
>>> (13/59)

The import is clear: Confucius's preoccupation is with order, and his order depends on the conduct of the wise prince. The few lines quoted above are in fact a free and, in a sense, truncated version of part of "The Text of Confucius," which Pound translated as follows.

Having attained this precise verbal definition [aliter, this sincerity], they then stabilized their hearts, they disciplined themselves: having attained self-discipline, they set their own houses in order; having order in their own homes, they brought good government to their own states; and when their states were well governed, the empire was brought into equilibrium.

From the Emperor, Son of Heaven, down to the common man, singly and all together, discipline is the root.

If the root be in confusion, nothing will be well governed.[7]

Pound also touched in this canto upon Confucius's doctrine of the mean and upon his call for moderation, although, radical and extreme to a fault, Pound must have found it hard "to stand firm in the middle."

In the same way in which Canto 13 comes in between the descriptions of the living hell, Canto 49 lightens up the dim world of *The Cantos* for a moment, tightly sandwiched as it is between the repulsive usury Cantos 45 and 51. Against the rush and bustle of the disorderly West, here are found some lyric vignettes, generating an unmistakable sense of quiet and tranquility. I find Pound's strategy here quite intriguing, as he invokes Li Po, the greatest Chinese lyric poet, to reinforce the impact he wishes to produce on the reader. Li's name is not mentioned, but a close scrutiny of the lines reveals a distinct poetic diction, image, and pathos which are peculiar to the Chinese poet.

I examine the two lines "Behind hill the Monk's bell / borne on the wind" as an illustration. These two lines seem to be a neat and effective compression of one Li Po poem. Of the few poems Li Po wrote about monks, the one entitled "On Hearing the Buddhist Priest of Shu Play His Table Lute" may have offered raw material for the Poundian lines.

> The priest of the province of Shu, carrying his
> table-lute in a cover of green, shot silk,
> Comes down the western slope of the peak of
> Mount Omei.

From these two lines we get the "monk" and the "hill."

> He moves his hands for me, striking the lute.
> It is like listening to the waters in ten
>   thousand ravines, and the wind in ten thousand
>   pine-trees,
> The traveller's heart is washed clean as in
>   flowering water.

And here we have a semblance of a "wind." Then the bell rings out its dulcet notes: "The echoes of the overtones join with the evening bell." We have still to look for the idea of "behind" somewhere, and it is near at hand:

> I am not conscious of the sunset behind the
>   jade-grey hill,
> Nor how many and dark are the autumn clouds.[8]

The ingredients are all there, and Pound's alchemic mind compounded them into the brief two lines in his Canto 49. The world as Li Po depicts it is one of order and peace (though not without grief and mishap), and he loves the beauty and serenity which he feels inheres in his universe. All through life Li Po traveled and saw a good deal of nature, with which he always feels at peace. This feeling of harmony and contentment informs his poetry, especially the poetry he wrote in the last few years of his life. Pound's invocation of his poetry and all that it implies counterpoints the sordidness and revulsion which the cantos preceding and following Canto 49 generate and helps to establish a larger framework for the bits and fragments that Pound included in his diverse work.

Meditating on exotic beauty and serenity, Pound recognized more than ever the validity and relevance of Confucius's notion of sage-kings. He must have felt an unusual exhilaration when he observed a scene of quiet and leisure:

> A light moves on the north sky line;
> where the young boys prod stones for shrimp.

In seventeen hundred [B.C.] came Tsing to these hill lakes.
A light moves on the south sky line.

(49/245)

The aura of the sage-ruler brightens up the whole of the universe. Working for the welfare of the people, such a ruler does not force people into debt and leave them to the mercy of usury. Hence the two ancient Chinese poems that follow, extolling the virtues of the beloved monarchs. The first is a eulogy, traditionally attributed to the period of Emperor Shun, as Angela Jung points out.[9] This poem likens the enlightening rule of the legendary king to the light of the sun and the moon and expresses the popular desire that such reign continue, as the sun returns day after day. From the second poem springs, among other things, a sense of the people's contentment with living in an age of peace and harmony when no taxes or tyranny harassed their simple agrarian life.

From these poems we now arrive at the inscrutable concluding lines of the canto:

The fourth; the dimension of stillness.
And the power over wild beasts.

(49/245)

The mood is still Confucian. The Chinese philosopher holds that to rule by virtue is to sit still and do nothing, as did Emperor Shun, and the founder of the Shang dynasty who "considered the people's sweats and sat calm on the throne" (Canto 53).[10] Virtue is always apotheosized and even mystified in Confucian classics as a force assuming an almost supernatural dimension and generating powers no human effort can achieve. In this fourth, or superhuman, dimension, virtue leads to order and harmony, and order and harmony in turn endow virtue with a divine ennobling and civilizing power. Seen in this perspective, Canto 49 looks backward to echo an earlier note in Canto 13 and ahead past the two disturbing intervening cantos to the China cantos sequence. When the poet finishes taking stock of his delinquent, straying forties and returns to sanity through repentance and suffering in the *Pisan Cantos*, he will allow the proper spirit of Canto 49 to reassert itself in his final glimpse of the earthly paradise in *Rock-Drill* and *Thrones*. Canto 49, appearing about in the middle of the whole epic, thus provides the disparate fragments of *The Cantos* with a meaning and purpose for their being and protects them against a confusion which does not seem to end with the arbitrary conclusion of the epic.

Based on the Confucian classic *Li Ki*, Canto 52 reads like an account of astrological movements and changes of seasons, seemingly out of tune with the rest of the cantos. Why is the sun, moving along a sign of the zodiac, in *The Cantos*? Or why review the cyclic operations of nature? Everything falls into place, however, under the concept *order*, the condition which *The Cantos* aim at establishing. People need ritual and ceremony to impart a sense of order to their universe. They need to revere the lords of mountains and great rivers because these provide a frame of reference for their conduct. They need to accustom themselves to the routines of the seasons because these delimit and regulate their lives. Order inheres in nature. As people tend toward disorder, nature acts as a safety valve for them. The picture of humans, beasts, and their world moving in harmony thus acquires a quality of timelessness and placelessness and serves as a corrective to the discord that Pound senses is spreading in the West. Moreover, the cyclic quality of the seasons in a way suggests the schema of the China cantos: dynasties wax and wane, empires coalesce and cleave asunder. Canto 52 is thus a proper introduction to the whole of the China cantos sequence.

In more ways than one, the Poundian statement "at the center of every movement for order there is a Confucian" provides a paradigm for the China cantos and for the cantos about John Adams's America.[11] Here we see the poet-historian (more poet than historian, considering his gross inaccuracies and occasional transpositions in his presentation of history), like King Cyrus of Persia, sitting on top of a hill, watching the endless pageant of events and people, meditating on the incessant rise and fall of fortunes below, and trying to discern a universal pattern. Pound thought he found one. And indeed, he did, although the copyright is not exclusively his. It is essentially Confucius's "a good governor is as wind over grass." In his "a good ruler keeps down taxes" (53/267), Pound quotes Confucius. The first part of the quotation stresses the idea of virtue, and the second, that of taxation, which is related to economics and possibly usury. The virtue-taxation formula becomes Pound's one yardstick for evaluating history. A virtuous ruler, who carefully oversees taxes, is awarded with peace and order.

Skipping over long periods of history in which such human benefactors as Yao, Shun, and Yu performed their legendary deeds, Pound first takes us to the reign of Tching-ouang (Emperor Cheng of Chou), who kept peace in the empire all his life by keeping "lynx eye on bureaucrats / lynx eye on the *currency*" (53/267, emphasis added). One of the prerequisites for being the lord over the "four seas of China" is, as a descendant of the Duke of Chou puts it, to "let the poor speak evil of taxes" (53/270). The House of Chou thrived for a few centuries on the diligent labors of its first builders, until its descendants, becoming either interested in hunting "across the tilled fields" or "avid of silver" (53/270), reduced it to ruin and destruction. Bloody murders and treasons followed in quick succession, and order gave way to usurpations, jealousies, and heavy taxes.

Extremes provoke a reaction. At the end of chaos is the blessing of order and peace. To Pound, all things pivot on the virtue-taxation formula. On the debris of the short-lived Chin dynasty, which savagely burnt Confucian books and scholars alike, Lieou Pang (Liu Pang) manages to erect the edifice of the Hans. He established the doctrine of Confucius as the ruling orthodoxy of the empire "and brought calm and abundance / No taxes for a whole year," so "men / sung of peace and of empire" in his day. But history repeated itself four centuries later. With the monarchs leaving the Confucian way, taxes rose, which led to war and oppression, and the confusion that ensued as a logical corollary left the Hans in disgrace and desolation. The transient House of the Souis (Suis) added to the prevailing chaos, until the founder of the T'ang Dynasty brought wise rule back to the kingdom. Under his rule, "Kung is to China as is water to fishes" (54/285). One of his successors brought down prices, and another levied no taxes for a period of five years in a famine-stricken locality. However, when the rulers started to "do nothing but think up new novelties" to suck the land dry, the T'angs were doomed. The empire was thrown into disorder once more.

The first king of the Sungs "reviewed all capital sentences / took tax power from governors" (55/294). But the greed of his scion soon discredited his efforts and brought on a revolt of the people, who cried out for just distribution. The reform of Ouang Ngan-che (Wang An-shi), resetting market tribunals and aiding a ruined agrarian economy, brought only temporary relief and proved a failure in its attempt to revive the shattered fortunes of the dynasty. As Pound sees it, "SUNG |sic| died of taxes and gim-cracks" (55/299). The Mongols who took over from the Sungs were "fallen / from losing the law of Chung Ni |Confucius|" (56/308).

The seventeenth century saw the Tartars on the Chinese throne. Such was the refining power of Confucianism that the "barbarians" civilized themselves with it and brought order back to a war-infected land (Canto 58). "Urbanity in externals, virtù in internals" (59/324), the Manchu princes were in concord and favored "no usury" (60/329). Emperor Young Tching ordered to

> prepare a total anatomy, et
> qu'ils veillerent à la pureté du langage

>   et qu'on n'employat que des termes propres
>   (namely Ch'ing ming)
>   (60/332–33)

Alternatively, "call pork pork" (61/336). From Kien-Long's (Chien Lung's) sixty-year-long reign, the one thing that stands out and redounds to his credit is the fact that he "exempted his empire from the land tax / for a year" (61/340). We thus come to the end of a highly idiosyncratic, simplistic, and idealistic presentation of Chinese history. Since much has been written on the Adams cantos as related to the Chinese sequence, I simply agree here with Pound that "there is Western thought that conforms to Confucius'." The career of John Adams and other early American leaders, their integrity and their justice, embodied for Pound the finest virtues of the early national period.[12]

In a sense the *Rock-Drill* and *Thrones* sequences continue the theme treated in the China cantos. The first of these dwells more on usury, and the second, more on eulogizing virtuous rulers, but neither deviates much from the general thematic pattern of the China cantos. "Canto 85 is," Pound says in a footnote attached to the canto, "a somewhat detailed confirmation of Kung's [Confucius's] view that the basic principles of government are found in the *Shu*, the History Classic" (85/559). On the whole a liberal rendering of *The Book of History*, the canto continues the note of eulogizing virtuous rulers and good government. The opening of the canto refers to the founding emperors of the Chou dynasty, King Wen and King Wu, who, on account of their virtue, received the decree of heaven to rule. Then the poet looked some six hundred years back at the deeds of a good Shang minister, Yi Yin, who referred his young king to the virtues of the king's grandfather, Cheng T'ang, in order to make him into a good and wise monarch. The pronounced emphasis on virtue in these cantos is further evidenced by the recurrence of the Chinese characters *te* ("virtue") and *jiao* ("to teach") and by the injunction.

Not serendipity
but to spread

tê
Thru the people.
(85/548)

After all, the decree of heaven "could extend to the people's
subsidia, / that it was in some fine way tied up with the people." For a ruler to be constantly aware of this truth and to
practice true virtue reposes his heart and makes it better every
day, as *The Book of History* says.

Canto 86 provides a synopsis of European history but is
nevertheless Confucian in theme. Not only are there many
interpolations of Chinese characters in between statements by
or about Bismarck and Talleyrand, a quick look at Babylon, and
a poignant thrust at F. D. Roosevelt, but the character for the
cardinal Confucian virtue, compassion, opens and pervades
the whole canto. And such is its force that:

WITH solicitude

恤

that mirroured turbationem,
Bismark forgotten, fantasia without balance-wheel,
"No more wars after '70" (Bismarck.)
"Dummheit, nicht Bosheit," said old Margherita
            (or Elenor? dowager)
"Sono tutti eretici, Santo Padro,
            ma non sono cattivi."
Mind (the kaiser's) like loose dice in a box.
Ballin said: "If I had known,
        wd / indeed have stuffed all Hamburg with grain."
(86/560)

The quotations from Bismark, Margaret of Savoia, and Albert Reader Ballin all reveal the theme of benevolence which informs the lines here. Then after a brief mention of Talleyrand's political strategies, more Chinese characters intervene and with them the Confucian comments "lost the feel of the people" and "way repeatedly not clean, noisy, and your hearts loveless."[13] In one section of the canto, we hear Mou Wang (King Mu of Chou) admonishing his successor on the love of loyalty and sincerity, and in another we read of the faithless and dishonest King Jou (King You, the last of the line of Western Chou) "killed by barbarians."

Pound reflects an obvious Confucian aversion against molesting the people with unnecessary and avoidable aggravation. Pound did not forget his concern with usury. " 'What' (Cato speaking) 'do you think of murder?' " This line is cryptic. It brings to mind the whole of Pound's essay "Gold and Work." There he says, "Usury is a vice or a crime condemned by all religions and by every ancient moralist." Quoting Cato, he continues, "For example, in Cato's *De Re Rustica* we find the following piece of dialogue: 'And what do you think of usury?' 'What do you think of murder?' "[14] Usury is equated with murder in *The Cantos* as well as in this essay. I note here only that to see usury as the root of all evil and then to hate the Jews exhibits at once Pound's naive, simplistic approach to evil and his own crass ignorance about human society.

The theme of usury is prominent in the next canto, which opens, as Bacigalupo puts it, with a clumsy effort to define it:

> . . . between the usurer and any man who
>   wants to do a good job
>   (perenne)
>   without regard to production—
>   a charge
>   for the use of money or credit.
>   (87/569)

To Pound "the problem of issue" consists in "attention to out-
let, no attention to source," so that "infantilism |increases| till
our time" and "paideuma |fades|" (87). For the idea "without
regard to production," Pound had "the great chapter, Mencius,
III, i, III, 6" in mind: "Nowt better than share (Mencius) / nor
worse than a fixed charge," or as he further telescopes the
notion in Canto 99, "a share, not a fixed charge" (99/698). "The
great chapter" is in fact a record of two conversations of Mencius, one with T'ang Wan Kung (Duke Wan of the state of T'ang),
and one with the duke's adviser, Peih Chen. It centers on government and taxation. Having warned the duke that "he who
seeks to be rich will not be benevolent," Mencius proceeds to
summarize the economic history of China's first three dynasties—Hea, Shang, and Chou.[15] As he sees it, two economic
systems were in practice then, namely, the share system and the
aid system, under both of which the people paid a tithe.

Mencius concludes this part of his discourse with the duke
by saying, "For regulating the lands, there is no better system
than that of mutual aid, and none which is not better than that
of taxing. By the tax system, the regular amount was fixed by
taking the average of several years (which in bad years causes
famine)." The emphasis is on benevolent rule and care for the
people. Pound's line "Nowt better than share (Mencius)" is, as
the quotation above shows, a slight distortion of Mencius's
preference for the mutual-aid system.

Mencius detests the word *profit*. He favors *benevolence and righteousness*. In an audience with a king he begins his discussion of
statecraft by picking a quarrel (and Mencius was as querulous
as Pound was) with the king's use of the word. "Why must Your
Majesty use that word 'profit'? What I am 'likewise' provided
with, are counsels to benevolence and righteousness, and
these are my only topics." Mencius goes on to talk about the
evil effects of the word *profit* (Pound's etymological analysis of
the character yields a hazy "the grain cut" in the canto, without

telling us whether "the grain cut" is a good thing or not) and comes back full circle with what must have been an irritating admonition to the king: "Let Your Majesty also say, 'Benevolence and righteousness, and these shall be the only themes.' Why must you use that word—'profit'?" We have noted the repetitious—hence emphatic—use of the word *only*, both at the beginning and at the conclusion of the conversation. It portrays an anxious Mencius trying to stress to the king the point that one can not set one's mind on "profit" and be a good ruler at the same time. Here there is no middle road to steer. Thus in the canto we read:

> "Why must say profit
>
> 利   (the grain cut).
>
> No dichotomy.
>
>   (87/575)

It is only natural that a few lines later we find Pound murmuring "or even the use of process? / That fine old word." The term *process* has always been Pound's equivalent for the Confucian *Tao*, which is attainable only through accumulation of acts of benevolence and righteousness. And if we assume that the word came into currency in the sense of "the way of heaven" in the time of Confucius or a little earlier, it was by Pound's day well over 2,500 years old.

The voice of Mencius still rings in Pound's ear when he goes on, inadvertently perhaps, to immortalize Thomas Hart Benton's chronicle of America (1820–50) in the American diptych, Cantos 88 and 89. Using irony to disparage the American banking system as a form of usury against the people, Pound brings Mencius's "great chapter" into Canto 88. Here, against a detailed account of Randolph's transaction with the bank, the casual line "Mencius on tithing" appears. Brief as it is, the poet knows full well that it carries enough import to throw his economic ideal into relief against the bleak background of American banking monopolies. Earlier I mentioned Mencius's conversation with an adviser of Duke Wan of the state of T'ang. Here the Chinese philosopher-statesman elaborated his notion of paying a tithe, as "the nine-square land system." Under this system, land is cut into nine equal divisions, the central square of which is to be cultivated on mutual aid for the state, and the people pay a tenth part of their produce. In this way Mencius envisioned achieving the ideal of even distribution. Pound embraced this principle in his strenuous fight against usury.

Pound can be shamelessly repetitious. Canto 89 shows a garrulous aging man stepping up his never-ending condemnation of the evil monetary system in force everywhere in Europe and America:

> Filled France with precious metals,
> when England with her overgrown bank . . .
> and France had no mines for these metals.
> Public debt increased (England) 400 million.
> Debt born of the Bank of England.
> (89/591)

As a result, "Every citizen [is] more or less cheated." Furthermore, "The government ceases to be independent / when currency is at will of a company" (89/594), echoing earlier lines, "such / a bank tends to subjugate government" (88/586) and "Without historic black-out / they can not maintain perpetual wars" (89/595). Pound sees "The civil war rooted in tariff" (89/596). Against this "historic black-out," Pound sees an illumination in

> China, the longest, and with the lowest percent
> of burocracy [sic].
> "200 years," said the Emperor, "and no trouble."
> (89/599)

It does not matter much that this account is far from a true representation of the political and economic history of China. For our discussion here, it is important that Pound sees an ideal there which he regards as an antidote to the anti-ideal, the sordid mundane reality. In the way in which Canto 13 flickers against the gloom of the hell cantos and Canto 49 glimmers through the somber universe of *The Cantos* as a whole, the brief "Mencius on tithing" thus helps to dispel, in a manner of speaking, the oppressive atmosphere which the massive account of the American banking practice (usury) creates.

As Pound himself points out, *Thrones* concerns the states of mind of people responsible for something more than their personal conduct.[16]

> Sage men have plans,
> simplicity a thousand generations, no man can change.
> The Sage Emperor's heart is our heart,
> His government is our government
>   yao^2 high, hsiao^3 dawn
> The Venerated Emperor
>   watched things grow with affection.
>   (99/695)

These lines establish the principle which governs Pound's selection of sage-kings to put in *Thrones*, in fact a gallery of responsible leaders taken out of civilizations as diverse as Rome, Byzantium, China, and England, and endowed with an earthly immortality. Mons of Jute, Justinian the Great, Diocletian, Vespasian, Antonius, Heraclius, Authar, Charlemagne, Canute, Edward III, and many others take their rightful places in the hall of fame.

The Chinese diptych in this sequence, Cantos 98 and 99, recounting the royal edicts of the enlightened Manchu emperors Kang Hsi and his successor Iong Cheng (Yung Cheng), is intended to provide an outline of Confucius's political doctrine. Canto 98 is an overview and Canto 99 an elaboration, the diptych ending with an enthusiastic acclamation of the king and his consort. The sixteen edicts of Emperor Kang Hsi, viewed in their totality, repeat two basic Confucian theories regarding government, namely, to teach the people to be good and to care for them. The people should be educated to be "gentlemen," to love filial piety, to be natural ("no need of contraptions"), and to keep peace and order ("avoid litigations"). For its own part the state should define the law and enforce it well and see to it that the people are well settled and happy in their trades and occupations, free from "a fixed charge" of taxation ("Taxes, for public utility, / a share of a product" |9/705|). It all sounds like an ideal social contract—which Kang Hsi's regime was not.

Emperor Iong Cheng received and enlarged on his father's injunctions; but the basic concern remains the same: virtue on the part of the ruler and order and food for the people.

> |The king's| job was the swan's flight (hung^2 yeah$^{4-5}$)
> To trace out and to bind together
> From sonship this goes to clan
> and to avoid litigations
> > out of the field, from the trees,
> Food is the root.
> > Feed the people (99/695).
> ·
> > Let a man do a good job at his trade,
> > > whence is honesty;
> > > whence are good manners,
> > > > good custom
> > > this is tuan^1 cheng^4
> > > > good living.
> > > > > (99/700)

We find that the virtues stressed here are basically the same as those illustrated in *The Book of Poetry* and other Confucian classics: gentility, sincerity, and justice for the people.

> Laws must be for the general good,
>   for the people's uprightness,
>   their moral uprightness.
> . . . .
>   a gentleman's job is his sincerity.
> . . . .
> Not to lie out of heedlessness
>   let alone out of trickery.
>   (99/697, 705)

The king must act upon the basic belief that "man's phallic heart is from heaven / a clear spring of rightness" (99/697) and that "a man's paradise is his good nature" (99/699). On the king the fate of the empire hinges ("The whole tribe is from one man's body / What other way can you think of it?" |99/708|). And the ideal society is one in which compassion reigns supreme and order and accord prevails:

> Small birds sing in chorus,
> Harmony is in the proportion of the branches
>   as clarity (chao[1]).
> Compassion, tree's root and water-spring;
>   The state: order, inside a boundary;
>   Law: reciprocity.
> What is statute save reciprocity?
> One village in order,
>   one valley will reach the four seas.
>   (99/708)

The last two lines bring us right back to the basic Confucian principle that, when the individual is perfect, an ideal social order will follow. These lines also remind us of Pound's diagnosis of the disease affecting America and the West, a diagnosis which led him to see the wisdom and sanity of Confucianism and accept it as the panacea he had been looking for. "The drear horror of American life," Pound wrote some time toward the end of the 1920s, can be traced to two damnable roots, or perhaps it is only one root: 1. The loss of all distinction between public and private affairs. 2. The tendency to mess into other people's affairs before establishing order in one's own affairs, and in one's thought. To which one might perhaps add the lack of any habit in America of connecting or correlating *any* act or thought to *any* main principle whatsoever, the ineffable rudderlessness of that people. The principle of good is enunciated by Confucius: it consists in establishing order within oneself. This order or harmony spreads by a sort of contagion without specific effort.[17]

Believing that in his quest for the rudder and the principle he had found them in Confucius's doctrine, he answered Eliot's question, "What does Mr. Pound believe?" in his self-confident and unequivocal tone in 1934: "I believe the *Ta Hio* [the Great Learning]."[18] As we have noted, in this Confucian classic Confucius formulated his ideal ethical and political pattern for individual, state, and kingdom. In many senses our discussion thus comes full circle.

Pound was a visionary artist. To his credit he felt that humanity deserves better than it gets, and it deserves the best.[19] He saw a chaotic world that needed setting to rights and a humanity, suffering from spiritual dearth and cosmic injustice, who needed to be saved. Anxious to stop the tottering Western civilization from going under, he ransacked history for long-lost ideals and principles from the golden past. He set out to achieve nothing short of a cultural synthesis, a new paideuma, which would teach people how to relate themselves to the world, how to overcome alienation, and how to control their own destiny. He would write a poem which would make the reader a new person, a whole person at home in the world. With this arduous messianic program to execute and this next-to-divine responsibility to discharge, Pound, like Eliot, struggled in the desert.[20] And, like Blake, he stood before hellmouth, "Shouting, whirling his arms, the swift limbs, / Howling against evil" (16/68).

Nostalgia for the ideal past, desire to salvage a world from total decay, and devotion to humanity proved to be the bonds that tied him and Confucius together. Whether for good or for evil, rightly or wrongly, Pound was for the most part of his life trying to offer Confucian philosophy as the one faith which could help him save the West. Anyone good in his eyes was a Confucian: Sigismondo Malatesta, Andrew Jackson, the Adamses, and ancient rulers resurrected from various civilizations of the distant past. Anything good in his opinion illustrated some Confucian virtue. *The Cantos*, thematically as well as formally, are a diversity, and it would be hard to fit this sprawling colossus neatly into any one framework. Nevertheless, if we choose to see Confucius's philosophy on ethics, politics, and economics as the thread stringing the disparate beads of the hundred-odd cantos together, then we can without exaggeration state that Confucius may have been the guiding spirit for Pound in his writing of *The Cantos*.

The influence of Confucius's philosophy on Pound is not always fortunate and wholesome. There are certain unhealthy tendencies in the Confucian classics which may have echoed and strengthened similar propensities in Pound. One such issue relates to race and racial discrimination. Obviously chauvinistic, Confucius spoke of minority nationalities in outlying areas of China only as barbarians. "The barbarian tribes of the east and the north, even though they have princes to lead them, are not half as well governed as those states of our great land without the benefit of princely leadership," he said on one occasion.[21] And we find Pound speaking in *The Cantos* in the same contemptuous tone of the "crude tribes of the north" (the Mongols) as "mongrels":

> this was a new idea to the mongols
> who wanted to turn all land into grazing
>   and saw no use for human inhabitants
> these mongrels bein' 'orseman.
>   (55/300)

And he called northeast tribes "savages and hordes":

> And on t'other side was the question of horse fairs, and tartars
> of whom were Nutche or savage,
>   these traded at Kaiyuen
> and the other great hordes, Pe and Nan-Koan
>   that were beyond the great wall fighting each other.
>   (58/317)

On another occasion, while talking about the contribution of Kwang Chung, an ancient statesman, to the Chinese civilization, Confucius says, "But for Kwang Chung, we should now be wearing our hair unbound, and the lappets of our coats buttoning on the left side," as the minorities were wont to do.[22] And we hear Pound saying in his *Rock Drill* sequence, "Quis erudiet without documenta? / even barbarians who button their coats t'other way on. / Non periturum" (86/561). We naturally think of Pound's indulgent and undisguised contempt for the Jewish people.

> Remarked Ben: better keep out the jews
> or yr/grand children will curse you
> jews, real jews, chazims, and neschek
> also super-neschek or the international racket.
>   (52/257)

Pound's contempt amounts almost to hatred, although he claims to have neither prejudice nor hatred.[23] How much is Confucian influence on Pound's racial prejudice is hard to ascertain. Massimo Bacigalupo traces Pound's espousal of anti-Semitism to his family and social background:

> The family fortunes had been waning. And we know from Pound's biographers that as a boy he was painfully aware that some of his friends were better off. Eventually he came to believe, like other members of his class, that his impoverishment (the consequence of competitive capitalism) was due to the waves of immigrants who could be seen thriving in their "vulgar-

ity," and perverting the pristine American stock. Hence his contemptuous attitude to minorities, particularly to Jews.[24]

Related to his racial prejudice is Pound's adamant condemnation of usury as the root of all evil. Pound's overriding
concern with economics is most unfortunate, in more ways
than one. He wrote in 1937, "We are bedevilled with false diagnosis. We are obfuscated with the noise of those who attribute
all troubles to irrelevant symptoms of evil." His own diagnosis
of the social disease of his times is nothing but false, and usury
is merely a symptom of evil—an irrelevant one at that, as
George P. Elliot points out.[25]

Moreover, from his analysis of usury he concludes that distribution is the only alternative to monopoly ("Good sovereign
by distribution / Evil king is known by his imposts" [52/261]).
He regards Mencius's "great chapter" as great because the Chinese philosopher favors the principle of "even distribution,"
and the line "T'ang opened the copper mine" stands in Canto
88 because the ancient Chinese king understood "the dis-
tributive function of money." This preoccupation with "distribution" as an ideal may have pushed Pound some way toward
accepting Mussolini's program in Italy and blinded him to the
brutalities which that regime committed there, not to mention
that the Cantos 72 and 73 are a kind of celebration of the Fascist
final days of terror in northern Italy.[26] Of course, Pound could
well have been on the side of America. For who could tell what
effect it would have had on a sensitive Pound had President
Roosevelt at least listened to his economic program, particularly since Pound returned to his native country nineteen
years after he left it only for the reason of selling his reform
package first to America? As it was, Roosevelt was too busy for
the babble of a visionary man of letters, and the frustrated and
indignant Pound turned instead to the wrong man, Mussolini
and his Fascist Italy. I do not mean to exonerate Pound from his
grave error of judgment; I simply point out how much Pound's
sanity depended on his economic idea.[27]

As we have indicated earlier, Confucius's emphasis on the importance of the virtuous prince could easily, as it actually did in feudal China, lend support to authoritarianism. As early as Canto 8 we read such disturbing lines as

> And telling of how Plato went to Dionysius of Syracuse
> Because he had observed that tyrants
> Were most efficient in all that they set their hands to.
>
> (8/31)

The subsequent series of idealized portrayals of kings and emperors, Chinese or otherwise, certainly bespeaks Pound's endorsement of dictatorship. This attitude led to his support of Fascism, an act which has been neither forgotten nor forgiven and has possibly left an indelible stigma on his name.

Works of art, once completed, acquire an independent existence and invite interpretations which may not always have much to do with their creators. To say that a person with bad political ideas cannot write good poetry and thus condemn both Pound and his masterwork is perhaps as simplistic as to dismiss Wagner's music as worthless, on the basis of a judgment about Wagner personally.[28] At the beginning of this chapter, I touched briefly upon the sense of mission with which Pound embarked on his poetic career. As he says of John Adams, the "aim of my life has been to be useful" (70/412). If, toward the end of his cantos, his earthly paradise is still in the making, he has at least tried for the little light and harmony, for "a little light, like a rushlight" (116/797) can lead back to splendor.[29] The motives of his struggles and the validity of his outlook have been duly recognized. Drawing attention to the idealistic and honorable tradition of Pound's thinking on economics but soberly aware of his stained record in these matters, M. L. Rosenthal offers what seems to be a balanced view of Pound's behavior:

> In the face of these imponderables and of his own insufferable dogmatism, we are compelled to recognize in his poetry at its

best, the humane motives and the moral and intellectual power of his essential outlook. It is then, we feel, that he is a child of the enlightenment after all, of Voltaire and the encyclopaedists, and that his satires and harangues are quite something else than special pleading for a vicious thought and behaviour.[30]

Through the ordeal at the Disciplinary Training Center at Pisa and in St. Elizabeths Hospital in Washington, D.C., the poet learned humility and compassion and offers, among other things, a repentance in his *Pisan Cantos* and other later sequences. "I am noman, my name is noman," "a man on whom the sun has gone down" (74/426, 431). "Nothing counts save the quality of the affection" and that "the truth is in kindness" (77/466). And he did not forget the bitter lesson of the atrocious forties, when he says toward the end of Canto 117 and indeed also of the whole of *The Cantos*, "To be men not destroyers." It is somewhat pathetic to hear a man exhausted and defeated at the end of life's journey, uttering in plain desperation these lines:

> M'amour, m'amour
> > what do I love and
> > > where are you?
> That I lost my center
> > fighting the world.
> The dreams clash
> > and are shattered—
> and that I tried to make a paradiso
> > > > terrestre.
> > > (117/802)

He loved, dreamed, fought, and in a sense, failed. *The Cantos* are an indication that he meant well.

6

Pound and the Troubadours: Medieval and Modern Rebels

James J. Wilhelm

To appreciate Ezra Pound both as a scholar and as a rebel, we need only to look at his work with the troubadours of southern France. From the time he was a college student at Hamilton, Pound fell under the spell of these strange "singers of Provence," who, in the eyes of T. S. Eliot, were more remote to us today than the Sumerians. But to Pound, who took the time and trouble to study them, the troubadours were anything but remote. They were persistent itinerant preachers of love, precisely as our modern rock singers are today, and they both fascinated and, to a degree, irritated the society about them precisely the way Madonna or Boy George does today. Their names, in fact—Marcabrun, or Dark Spot, Cercamon, or Search-the-World—often conveyed the same eccentric natures we see in our own songsters. They were, in short, rebels with lyres, and their cause was the promotion of love.

Pound always viewed the troubadours as iconoclastic groundbreakers in the fields of both love and poetry. He knew that the name *trobaire* descends from the Provençal verb *trobar,* "to invent, to find." It stems ultimately from the Latin word

tropus, related to the Greek *trephein*, and means a "turning"—
either of thought or expression. The emphasis is on originality
and change, not on a static or fixed concept. Unfortunately,
many of our scholars today view these poets through the eyes
of French structuralism, which tends to reduce their individual
compositions to mere copies of a general form that pervades
the period from 1100 to 1225, when troubadour poetry was at
its height. These scholars want to know what "the alba" consists of; they are not much interested in any one dawn song,
some of which Pound translated. They also concentrate on a
fixed or standard vocabulary that one can observe in many
compositions, those endlessly positivistic terms that appear
again and again; the lady is usually "beautiful, genteel, cour-
teous, noble," and so on ad infinitum. In short, the troubadours
are simply praisers of love, interesting not so much in and of
themselves as because they were the precursors of Dante and
his circle, who were the precursors of Petrarch, who is the father
of the sonnet—which Ezra Pound thought was a boring and
perniciously pervasive art form that had achieved far too much
notice in Western culture. By contrast, Pound as a poet and
translator was interested in the poets' differences: the unusual
way that Bertran de Born voices a masculine poetry or that
Peire Cardenal criticizes the church. As an artist striving to find
his own voice, he emphasized the troubadours' originality even
during his college days, when he examined a highly intricate
poem of Guiraut de Bornelh and tried to imitate the rhymes.[1]
Unlike the structuralists, Pound was interested in the one, not
the many.

While Pound was studying at Hamilton under the guidance
of the renowned Provençalist William P. Shepard, he stumbled
on the most difficult and ingenious of all these songwriters,
Arnaut Daniel, whom he later translated. Pound's road into
troubadour land had been charted by the great Dante Alighieri,
whose treatise on poetry the *De vulgari eloquentia* (On popular
eloquence) Pound revered. Pound scrupulously studied

Dante's samples from the troubadours, trying to determine what Dante saw in these earlier writers. Neither Dante nor Pound was interested in any sameness here; they saw magnificent inventiveness, a return to song and melody after about eight centuries of silence, during which little love poetry was written in Europe. To both Dante and Pound, the troubadours were songbirds who had returned after a long and arduous winter, and their voices were often unique, as different as the sound of a lark is from that of a thrush or a swallow. It is not an accident that Pound in *The Cantos* repeatedly mentions the names of birds. In the very brief Canto 75, he prints the music of *Chant des oiseaux* (Song of the birds), by the French composer Jannequin, for he saw Jannequin as a later French manifestation of the earlier troubadour beginning.

Why study the troubadours? Clearly Dante and Pound would both say that one studies them because they are the founders of modern poetry, but also because they brought a sense of Eros or Amor back to a Europe that had languished too long in the arms of a mystical Caritas, in which the supernatural had suppressed the natural. Pound expresses this idea very eloquently at the end of Canto 107, where he puts Dante and the medieval philosopher Ocellus with Confucius (Kung), the lawgiver Coke, and the scientist Agassiz:

> So that Dante's view is quite natural:
>   this light
>   as a river
>   in Kung; in Ocellus, Coke, Agassiz
>   *pei*, the flowing
>   this persistent awareness
> Three Ninas from Gaudier,
>   Their mania is a lusting for farness
>   Blind to the olive leaf,
>   not seeing the oak's veins.
>   (107/763)

The troubadours, who often began their love poems with

nature settings involving birds, plants, and flowers, are definitely a part of this tradition.[2]

I would like to consider now in more detail a poem as it is sung, the lovely "A chantar m'er de so qu'eu non volria," by the mysterious Countess of Dia. She is mysterious because the modern city of Die (ancient Dia) on the hills overlooking the Rhone Valley never had a countess—and even if it did have one, we still do not know her first name. The *vidas*, or life stories that often accompany the poems in the songbooks, provide mostly legendary "facts." This tradition tells us that the Countess, whom some called Beatrice (probably anticipating Dante), was in love with a lord of Poitiers (possibly the first troubadour, Guilhem of Poitiers); another tradition says that she loved Prince Raimbaut of Orange, a reckless noble who lived near Die. Both of these men were hellraisers and either could have inspired this song, which is what in the 1930s was called a "torch song."

I mention the shaky historical facts around the composition solely because when Pound was studying these works at Hamilton, he was fascinated by these legendary lives. He saw the troubadours not as faceless entities but as flesh-and-blood personalities who had lived lives that are every bit as romantic as their works. In fact, either alone or with his wife (and also with T. S. Eliot), he strolled the roads of southern France on foot, visiting the castles where the poets were believed to have lived. In his essay "Troubadours—Their Sorts and Conditions,"[3] he recounted many of the stories about these composers and performers, and he worked them into his early cantos. Pound felt that the body of myth surrounding these creators was similar to that which even in this technological age surrounds popular performers (we can think today of John Lennon or Elvis Presley). Pound walked from Ussel to Ventadorn to Excideuil, listening to the birds and studying the wave patterns sculpted into the walls. He saw the geniuses of the poets tied to the genius of place, and he felt a strong identification with both.[4]

In the Countess's song, I consider only the last two stanzas, where the *-ina* and *-atges* rhymes dominate. The Countess is trying to coax her unfaithful lover to come back to her, telling him that she will give him the perfect love that he desires and that no other woman in the world can compete with her in this respect. Billie Holliday was never more passionate or more forceful. Then, when the last stanza ends, she writes a little envoi, or short final stanza, where a few of the rhymes are repeated. (The *envoi* sends the song *en la via*, or out onto the road.) The poems circulated from castle to castle the way news items do today, and they were valued precisely because of their novelty and the way that they interrupted the general boredom of feudal life. Ezra Pound, living in capitalist societies, later wished that the cultures around him valued art half as much as these medieval lords and ladies did. Here are the countess's words:

> Proesa grans qu'el vostre cors s'aizina
> e lo rics pretz qu'avetz m'en ataina,
> c'una non sai, lonhdana ni vezina,
> si vol amar, vas vos no si'aclina;
> mas vos, amics, etz ben tant conoissens
> que ben devetz conoisser la plus fina;
> e membre vos de nostres partimens.
>
> Valer mi deu mos pretz e mos paratges,
> e ma beutatz e plus mos fis coratges,
> per qu'ieu vos man lai on es vostr'estages
> esta chansson que me sia messatges;
> e volh saber, lo mieus bels amics gens,
> per que vos m'etz tant fers ni tant salvatges;
> no sai si s'es orguoills o mal talens.
>
> Mas aitan plus volh li digas, messatges,
> qu'en trop d'orguolh an gran dan maintas gens.

In English translation:

> The great value that resides inside your form
> and the rich worth that you have upset me,

for I don't know any woman, far or near,
who doesn't incline toward you if she wants to love;
but you, my friend, are so completely discriminating
that you should know how to select the very finest;
and remember the poems of love (*or* partings) we made.

My own worth and noble lineage should have value,
as well as my beauty and, more, my refined emotions,
and so I send to you where your estate is
this song to serve as a messenger for me;
and I want to know, my handsome, charming friend,
why you're so fierce and cruel toward me;
I don't know if it's caused by pride or evil will.

But, my messenger, even more I want you to tell him
that with too much pride many people come to a loss.[5]

The music accompanying the song lacks any clear-cut guide-
lines for determining the rhythm. In one recording, the music
has an Andalusian orchestration, suggesting that there may be
some ties here with the Arabic compositions of southern
Spain.[6] This point is highly debatable, although Pound also
believed that the first troubadour, the aforementioned
Guilhem of Poitiers, or Poitou, "brought the song up out of
Spain" (Canto 8/32). Many people would argue this fact, simply
because Arabic music is not very similar to troubadour music
and because the cult of love as practiced among the Arabs,
where the women were kept in harems, did not seem to have
the liberating effect that it had in France. Also, a great deal of
Arabic poetry is homosexual, which is not typical of troubadour verse. The women often have masculine names, which
seems to occur because the men are insisting that the ladies
are their equal; hence they masculinize their names and call
them "milord." Even the Roman poet Ovid, who scarcely meant
it literally, said that his lady was his master, and the "prisoner of
love" motif runs throughout our own popular songs.[7]
    The mention of bondage or rendering homage to a woman

brings up the banal term *courtly love*, a modern phrase that no one has yet satisfactorily defined. For the troubadours to have called their love *cortes* would have suggested etiquette, good manners, and proper behavior. Yet passion, not courtesy per se, is their primary concern. The majority of the finest troubadour poems are emotional. Elsewhere, for example, the Countess says the following:

> I've suffered great distress
> From a knight whom I once owned.
> Now, for all time, be it known:
> I loved him—yes, to excess.
>   His jilting I've regretted,
> Yet his love I never really returned.
> Now for my sin I can only burn:
> Dressed, or in my bed.
>
> O, if I had the knight to caress
> Naked all night in my arms,
> He'd be ravished by the charm
> Of using, for cushion, my breast.
>   His love I more deeply prize
> Than Floris did Blancheflor's.
> Take that love, my core,
>   My sense, my life, my eyes!
>
> Lovely lover, gracious, kind,
> When will I overcome your fight?
> O, if I could just lie with you one night—
> Feeling those loving lips on mine!
>   Listen, one thing sets me afire:
> Here in my husband's place I want *you*—
> If you'll just keep your promise true:
>   Give me every single thing I desire.[8]

The phrase *courtly love* (which sounds so pure and ceremonious, so unrelated to the boudoir) was invented two years before Ezra Pound was born, in 1883, by the French scholar

Gaston Paris. He wrote an article in the *Journal des savants* about Chretien de Troyes's famous romance *Lancelot*, which narrates the adulterous love of Lancelot for Guinevere. Paris noticed that the love affair in *Lancelot* was highly ritualized, almost like a religion, but it was dominated by a secular woman, Guinevere. He felt that, since this love was totally unlike anything ancient or modern, it required a new name, and so he coined the phrase *courtly love*. From the start, this term was popular because generic titles provide handy ways of describing things. From the start, however, the term could be seen as either positive or negative, since it concerned idealized adultery, and people who use it do not tend to be fully conscious of this ambiguity. To some people, courtly love is a magnificent social institution that leads ultimately to Dante's ethereal love for Beatrice. But to others, courtly love is a dangerous, sinful, adulterous pastime that led the south of France into the infamous Albigensian Crusade, when northern France, with the help of the Papacy, crushed the southerners under the guise of extirpating the dualist heresy known as Albigensianism.

It is quite possible, however, to read Provençal verse without using this humorless nineteenth-century tag, which, like structuralism, blurs the composers together into a faceless choir. Not all of the love affairs are adulterous, and some are not especially idealized. In short, the poetry is too rich and diversified to bear a single generic name. The tradition did not need a Linnaeus to catalog it; it needed an Ezra Pound to free it for the modern reader. Furthermore, the recurring tropes and metaphors are not especially medieval at all. The poet Cercamon says, "Love is sweet when it walks in / And bitter when it walks out."[9] Centuries before, on the island of Lesbos, Sappho had called love *glukupikron* ("sweet-bitter"), and in our own day the highly sophisticated lyricist Cole Porter said in "Get out of Town," "the thrill when we meet / is so bitter-sweet." Ultimately the term *courtly love* makes the poetry too spiritual, too easily plugged into Italian theology, too "safe." If troubadour verse had been "safe," it would never have been involved in the Albigensian Crusade, because after that infamous invasion, people in the south of France were prohibited from writing any love poetry except to the Virgin Mary.

The mention of things being not "safe" brings us directly to Ezra Pound. Of all the major writers of this century, he, more than any other, took the greatest risks, dared the most, lost the most, and even today is paying after his death for his egregious errors. This book, however, should testify that there were also some exceptional things that he did right. Although he was born in the nineteenth century, Pound rose above it. He never accepted the clichés of any period or person, with the unfortunate exception of Benito Mussolini. He seldom used the phrase *courtly love*. In fact, in his early *Spirit of Romance*, which appeared when he was only twenty-five years old, he suggested the term *chivalric love*, which conjures up the dangerous world of the knight more than the comfortable world of the court. For one thing, being a poet, and being especially a poet of masks or personae, he never believed that what a poem says literally should be taken as dogma. He never confused rhetoric with discursive statement. As a maker of images, he was a rhetorician and sometimes a manipulator of masks; as a broadcaster over Radio Rome, he was a propagandist. He was perfectly aware of the differences involved in the two modes.

Since Pound was born at the end of the Romantic Era, he regarded this movement with the same suspicions that he used in evaluating medieval romance. He was aware of the dangers inherent in both, just as Dante was never deceived into thinking that the high-blown sentiments of romantic love voiced by Tristan and Lancelot were noble expressions of pure love; Dante put these famous lovers in his Hell.[10] Being a child of the excesses of a decadent Romanticism, Pound tended to view his predecessors with extreme distrust; he was never overly fond of Richard Wagner, Alfred Tennyson, or any other latter-day worshipers of medieval romance such as Gaston

Paris. By 1912, in fact, he was prepared to lead the great re-
bellion of Classicism and control against Romanticism and
unchecked outpouring.

The troubadour who fascinated Pound the most and who
helped him prepare the way for modern literature was the difficult Arnaut Daniel.[11] Pound was working on Daniel in the fall of
1911, just before he got together with Richard Aldington and
Hilda Doolittle in a tea shop in Kensington or in the British
Museum and they issued their manifesto for the future. In
troubadour composition, there were, almost from the start, two
schools of verse: the easy (*pla*, or *leu*) and the hermetic, or
closed (*clus*). Even today, we can observe this cleft in our culture
between the popular and the intellectual, the highbrow and the
lowbrow. Both Arnaut and Ezra were members of the conservatives, who do not care to please the masses, although they
were extremely interested in preserving the high standards of
their art. Pound *did* write "The Ballad of the Goodly Fere," but he
then showed no desire to follow up on it; similarly, Arnaut's
poems were not as popular as some of his competitors', since
only two survive with music. Pound liked the way that Arnaut
put "craft" above everything, as the troubadour says in one of
his poems.

> Though this measure quaint confine me,
> And I chip out words and plane them,
>   They shall yet be true and clear
> When I finally have filed them.[12]

Arnaut and Ezra were in much the same position with relation to their respective cultures. Both were surrounded by fellow composers whom they regarded as slack, lazy, uninspired,
and amateurish. Both regarded the Establishments that faced
them as inimical or in need of change: Pound, the British
Empire; Arnaut, the Catholic Church and the Frankish kingdom
to the north that was threatening southern France. Both saw
love and poetry as two of the primary endeavors in life.

As I have already commented, Arnaut and the troubadours were great defenders of Amor, as was Ezra Pound. Although D. H. Lawrence has been given the major credit in this century for writing works that have freed us from the bondage of sexual repression, Ezra Pound should get some credit too. We live in a society today that enjoys great freedom, and we tend to forget the courage that it took seventy years ago to say anything remotely erotic. Consider Pound's *Lustra*, which was published in 1916 while World War I was raging. One might have thought that the war would have diverted the censors' attention, but it did not. The government was still upset over Lawrence's novel *The Rainbow*. When Ezra gave Elkin Mathews, his publisher, the copy for *Lustra* and Mathews foolishly passed it on to his printer without even reading the manuscript, the printer hastily sent the copy back and refused to set it. Mathews then told Pound that he found the following lines "nasty" or sometimes "very nasty."

> Go little naked and impudent songs,
> Go with a light foot! . . .
> Greet the grave and the stodgy,
> Salute them with your thumbs at your nose.

He objected to the opening of "The Temperaments":

> Nine adulteries, 12 liaisons, 64 fornications
> and something approaching a rape.

Mathews changed the title "Coitus" to "Pervigilium."[13] Even the delightful "Ancient Music," which parodies the Middle English "Summer is icumen in," was slated for omission. Yeats interceded to save some of the poems, but others did not appear as Pound wrote them until *Personae* of 1926, which was reissued with additions in 1949 by New Directions.

In many ways some of Arnaut's poems are more boldly suggestive than Pound's. In his famous sestina, which Pound translates only partially in his *Translations*,[14] Arnaut uses six end words, most of which are potentially lascivious. He uses a rod, which can be phallic; a chamber, which can be vaginal; the very suggestive verb *enter*; and even the word *arma*, which in Provençal can refer to soul, arms, weapons, or the genitals. Furthermore, one of the poems that most haunted Pound was Arnaut's *Doutz brais e critz*, which opens with a lovely spring setting and then moves into the bedroom, where the poem prays for an erotic vision:

> God, who did tax
>   not Longus' sin, respected
> That blind centurion beneath the spikes
> And him forgave, grant that we two shall lie
> Within one room, and seal therein our pact,
> Yes, that she kiss me in the half-light, leaning
> To me, and laugh and strip and stand forth in the lustre
> Where lamp-light with light limb but half engages.[15]

The last two lines are even more daring in the original, which I have translated in my edition of Arnaut as follows:

> That I may uncover her lovely body, playing and laughing,
> And I may contemplate her against the light of the lamp.[16]

Such talk was very potent in twelfth-century France, and it displeased the local bishops as much as Pound's poetry later displeased the censors of Georgian England. Yet neither poet gave up and allowed his puritanical culture to dominate him.

Of course Pound is most famous for the way that he freed modern verse from nineteenth-century strictures, and even here he had a friend in Arnaut Daniel. The majority of the composers of troubadour verse wrote in the same kind of predictable singsong beat that the inferior Victorian sonneteers and hymnologists used. When Pound decided to break this insidious heave of the pentameter, he went once again to Arnaut. Here is the first stanza of a poem that Pound translated.

The short, telegraphic lines forbid any kind of regular, lulling rhythm to develop:

> L'*aura amara*
> Fals *bruoills brancutz*
> Clarzir
> Quel *doutz espeissa ab fuoills,*
> Els *letz*
> Becs
> Dels *auzels ramencs*
> Ten *balps e mutz,*
> Pars
> E *non-pars;*
> Per qu'eu *m'esfortz*
> De *far e dir*
> Plazers
> A *mains per liei*
> Que m'a *virat bas d'aut,*
> Don tem *morir*
> Sils *afans no m'asoma.*

Pound brilliantly renders this stanza as follows:

> The bitter air
> Strips panoply
> From trees
> Where softer winds set leaves,
> And glad
> Beaks
> Now in brakes are coy,
> Scarce peep the wee
> Mates
> And un-mates.
>   What gaud's the work?
>   What good in the glees?
> What curse
> I strive to shake!

> Me hath she cast from high,
> In fell disease
> I lie, and deathly fearing.[17]

This poetry may not be free verse exactly, but it is certainly emancipated. Even when Arnaut is writing an apparently simple stanza in ordinary rhythm, he always employs caesuras and enjambments and breaks to prevent the metronome from taking over. This technique was surely one of the basic lessons that Pound learned from his Provençal master.

Here is a typical stanza of Arnaut's rendered by Pound into an English that shows a variety of rhythmic patterns:

> Now high and low, where leaves renew,
> Come buds on bough and spalliard pleach
> And no beak nor throat is muted;
> Auzel each in tune contrasted
> Letteth loose
> Wriblis spruce.
> Joy for them and spring would set
> Song on me, but Love assaileth
> Me and sets my words t'his dancing.[18]

Arnaut's major contribution to Pound's Imagism was the use of the poetic image in a heightened manner, the employment of the specific against the general. We have already cited one of Arnaut's most daring images as the figure of the nude woman standing by the candlelight. But there are many others. Pound was struck by Arnaut's saying that his lady had thrown a cloak of indigo over him and her to conceal their illicit love from nosy neighbors or by Arnaut's figure of using a chisel and a file to sculpt his songs. But the lines that one most remembers from Arnaut that stuck in Pound's mind were the ones with which he ends his song "Of the Trades and Love."[19] Here Arnaut, speaking out of the anonymity that many scholars would like to force on this poetry, insists on his identity; he chisels his name at the end of his poem, precisely as Adaminus de Sancto Giorgio inscribed his name on a beautiful pillar in the Church of San Zeno of Verona. Here we have Arnaut the rebel, standing up proudly against the culture that produced him, telling it that he refuses to be enslaved by its strictures. Pound often said that artists are the antennae of the race, and I believe that he had a poet like Arnaut in mind. In any case, I have no trouble in seeing two forward-looking artists here. The medieval one says:

> Ieu sui Arnautz, q'amas l'aura
> e chatz la lebre ab lo bou,
> e nadi contra suberna.

A modern counterpart might echo:

> I am Arnaut, who hoards the wind
> And chases the rabbit with the ox
> And swims against the swelling tide.[20]

7

Pound
as
Parodist

Leslie Fiedler

Everyone knows from childhood on what parody is. Certainly I remember (and I can hardly be unique in this regard) reciting parodies of certain school-anthology poems long before I had encountered the originals. Nonetheless, I feel compelled to begin—though I risk self-parody as a pedant thereby—with a pair of dictionary definitions that distinguish two meanings often blurred in our everyday usage of what is after all an ambiguous term. One kind of parody, which I shall refer to hereafter as intentional, perjorative parody, Webster defines as "a writing in which the language or style of an author is imitated for comic effect . . ."; while the other, which I shall henceforth call inadvertent, honorific (more properly, I suppose, would-be honorific) parody is described as "imitation that is faithful to a degree but that is weak, ridiculous or distorted." I am uncomfortably aware, however, that in the latter sense all writing which emulates or pays homage to an earlier model or aspires to establish its credentials as real canonical literature by evoking a tradition runs the risk of becoming parodic—is, I am tempted to say, willy-nilly, parodic or quasiparodic. Yet it took a long time before critics or writers became aware of this fact. Vergil, for instance, seems to have been blissfully unaware that there was anything funny about attempting to write—on order, and for pay—a Homeric Epic in the age of Augustus; as was Dante when he tried to write a Vergilian one—travestying a travesty, as it were, in the time of scholastic Christianity. Perhaps even Shakespeare did not suspect that his *Titus Andronicus* burlesques the Senecan horror drama which it seeks to emulate, though in the dying twentieth century it has become impossible, for some of us at least, to sit through that play with a straight face. This is because we are the heirs of Modernism, and our sensibilities are sharpened by poets and novelists defensively self-aware, which is to say, prepared to laugh at themselves before their readers laugh at them. The moment at which the founding fathers of Modernism triumphed was, it should be remembered, also the moment of the triumph of Mass Culture. Consequently, they could scarcely have remained unaware that the traditional High Culture of the West, of which they felt themselves to be the last alienated spokesmen (alienated from the great majority of their contemporaries precisely because of their nostalgia for that dying tradition), could be preserved even for the minority audience of their peers only if the great writers of the past who had established it were ironically undercut even as they were piously evoked. "These fragments I have shored against my ruins," is the classic phrase with which T. S. Eliot described the mode of honorific (a rather, perhaps, ambivalent, bipolar) parody by allusion and quotation central to his own poetic practice and to that of most other modernist masters as well. In *The Waste Land*, for instance, he echoes certain elegant anthology pieces, apparently all that is still recoverable of an admired but irrelevant cultural heritage: "So many I had not thought death had undone so many . . ."; "The Chair she sat on like a burnished throne . . ."; "Sweet Thames run softly till I sing my song . . ."; "When lovely woman stoops to folly . . ." By placing them in inappropriately banal and sordid contexts, he makes their very elegance seem a little absurd; thus managing simultaneously to satirize—however tenderly, lovingly—both those texts themselves, and—more brutally—the modern world of anomie and pop culture, in which not even he can any longer take them quite seriously.

At the same time, moreover, he also parodies pop culture itself, particularly the pop songs which most of the world in which he sought to make himself heard preferred not just to his own verse but to that of Dante and Spenser and Goldsmith and Shakespeare. "O O O O that Shakespearian rag. It's so elegant so intelligent . . ." an anonymous voice sings, parodying his evocation of the Bard. And we recall, as he apparently could not forget, that "The Love Song of J. Alfred Prufrock" and Irving Berlin's "Alexander's Ragtime Band" appeared at the same historical moment. But the bipolar parody of *The Waste Land* cuts deeper than that; since its very structure, what tenuous coherence and form it has, depends on an evocation with similar parodic intent of the archetypal tale of the Quest of the Holy Grail.

That pagan-Christian myth which in times when Europe was still both pagan and Christian, but in any case pious, possessed the deep imagination of both the courtly and folk audience, had, to be sure, not quite died in the secular, skeptical age into which Eliot was born. It persisted, however, chiefly in the nursery and the academy, in illustrated children's books and footnoted studies written by scholars for scholars. The debt of Eliot was chiefly to the latter, as the parodically pedantic footnotes which he appended to his poetic text make clear: confessing that the source of his inspiration was not the *Perceval* of Chretien de Troyes or Malory's *Morte D'Arthur*—much less Tennyson's *Idylls of the King*—but *The Golden Bough* of James Frazer and, especially, Jessie L. Weston's *From Ritual to Romance*.

So also Eliot's fellow High Modernist, James Joyce, plays in his mock epic *Ulysses* the game of bipolar parody by evoking

and travestying the archetypal story of the wanderings of Odysseus on his long way home. Not merely does he pathetically
translate the magic kingdoms of the Mediterranean into the
squalid urban environment of Dublin: but by suggesting that
the comic-pathetic, uncircumcised Jew, Leopold Bloom, is all
the Odysseus such a world can produce or afford, he also
insidiously suggests that perhaps his Homeric prototype may
have been nothing more. Thus he calls into question the very
notion not just of the Hero but of the Heroic Poem—perhaps
even of poetry itself, the Western tradition of which, after all,
begins with Homer. Some, indeed (including Joyce's brother,
Stanislaus), have contended that *Ulysses* as a whole must be
read as a travesty, a put-on or send-up not just of the myth of
Odysseus but also of the ironic book we hold in our hand and
of the notion of High Culture to which that book declares its
ironic allegiance.

   Not that Joyce (though in fact he consumed its products as
avidly as any shopgirl) takes popular culture quite seriously
either, mocking it, in fact, throughout *Ulysses*. He parodies, for
instance, in the "Nausicaa" episode the tone and diction of a
sentimental Victorian Ladies' best-seller called *The Lamplighter*,
a novel which—to compound the joke even more—almost
none of the academic critics of Joyce, who do not in general
share his taste for *schlock*, would be likely to recognize. But all of
them do, of course, recognize the English prose styles, ranging
from the Anglo-Saxon Chronicles to Dickens and beyond, trav-
estied in the "Oxen of the Sun" episode, that tour de force of
auto-parodic pedantry, which has become an occasion for further pedantry from those too learned to realize the joke is on
them.

   In any case, I would argue, travesty, parody, and burlesque
have been the hallmarks of Modernism from the start. It is,
therefore, scarcely surprising to discover that they are omni-
present in the poetry (and prose) of Ezra Pound, who is not
merely one of the key figures in, but an apologist for and pro-

moter of, that most self-conscious and self-advertised of all literary movements—its impressario-in-chief, as it were.

Pound is a parodist, however, not merely by virtue of his Modernism; but, even more perhaps, by virtue of his Americanism, for he is hopelessly, unredeemably American—more American by far than T. S. Eliot, as American as Whitman or Longfellow. And this (as I shall try eventually to make clear) not so much despite, as because of his long self-exile in Europe, and his shrill, almost hysterically declared allegiance to Old World culture; in presumed defense of which (as represented by Mussolini!), he risked imprisonment or death as a traitor to his own country. American poets, however, as W. H. Auden once contended, and I do in fact believe, are prone to inadvertent parody of a particular sort. "The danger of the American poet," Auden wrote, reflecting on the resemblances and even more conspicuous differences of a group of such poets which included William Carlos Williams, Vachel Lindsay, Marianne Moore, Wallace Stevens, E. E. Cummings, Laura Riding, and, of course, Pound, "is not that of writing like everybody else but of crankiness and a parody of his own manner."

The poets to whom Auden specifically refers belong to a single generation which came of age in the early twentieth century, and his observation is made in an attempt to define the differences between modernist verse in England and the United States. But, of course, American writers had been falling into the same trap even before the rise of Modernism, indeed, since the very beginnings of literature in English on this side of the Atlantic; and the reasons are obvious. We have never had a standard received literary tradition any more than we have had a standard received literary language. Our writers, therefore, have always had to invent and reinvent both—with, as T. S. Eliot puts it, "great labour," and they have all consequently run the risk (it is a source of their special charm, as well as their peculiar plight) of falling into ridiculous eccentricity.

Nor does it matter whether, like Poe and Melville and Longfellow, they have sought to construct a patchwork pseudo-tradi-
tion out of the scraps of European High Culture, which they
happened to know and love, or, like Whitman and Mark Twain,
they have opted for making an anti-tradition of tradi-
tionlessness. If the "barbaric yawp" of Whitman's *Leaves of Grass*,
with its vaunt of having canceled out all "old debts to Greece
and Rome" trembles eternally on the edge of self-travesty, so
also does Longfellow's *Hiawatha*, with its Indian lore dutifully
worked up out of scholarly sources and improbably rendered in
a meter borrowed from a Finnish Epic known in America only to
university professors. Both have, therefore, been more ultimately parodied (which is to say, pushed over that perilous
edge) ever since. In Longfellow's case, this has usually been
done with deliberate malice or condescension; in Whitman's,
most often inadvertently, in inept homage, as in the worst of
Carl Sandburg. Indeed, it is hard to emulate either of these two
laureates of mid-nineteenth-century America without falling,
willy-nilly, into burlesque. Yet Pound tried with both.

Longfellow, who was his great-uncle, he apparently despised
but could never quite manage to exorcize from his undermind.
In fact, though, as T. E. Lawrence once observed, he tried from
early adolescence to define for himself a life-style as diverse as
possible from that of his New England Brahmin ancestor; help-
lessly, hopelessly, he turned into a kind of unwitting caricature
of him: a University Professor of Comparative Literature (fired
from his first job, to be sure, for sharing his room with a trans-
vestite actress out of a traveling burlesque show) and an apos-
tle of hightone Old World Culture, which he translated from
many tongues for the benefit of his philistine compatriots who
spoke only their own. Moreover, impelled by God knows what
vestigial pieties, Pound published in 1913 what may well be the
only straightfaced imitation of *Hiawatha* in print, in which he
chants with, apparently, no sense of being ridiculous:

If you press me for the legend,
For the story of the maiden
Of the laughing Indian maiden
Of the radiant Minnehaha.

To be sure, as if to make up for this gaffe, he published some twenty or twenty-five years later, this time with malice aforethought, a parody of the best-known and most anthologized of his great-uncle's patriotic pieces, beginning, "Listen my children and you shall hear / The midnight activities of What's-his-name . . ." To this he attached, lest some obtuse reader fail to get the already obvious satirical point, an epigraph written, apparently by A. Orage, but surely at Pound's prompting: "Here's another improvement on a worn-out model. I did it very nearly in my sleep . . ."

Whitman, who seems to have haunted him waking, as Longfellow did him sleeping, Pound never either imitates so piously or caricatures so wickedly. Nevertheless, he does echo him over and over, even occasionally referring to him by name. As far as I know, however, no mainstream Poundian critic (perhaps because none of them has read Whitman hard and well) has ever dealt adequately with the equivocal but pervasive influence on the author of *The Cantos* of the author of *Leaves of Grass*, another unfinished, unfinishable, cranky, not-quite epic. But Pound himself, of course, had read Whitman hard and well from quite an early time, and he continued to wrestle all his life long with his oedipal ambivalence toward the older poet.

Even before he had publicly made peace with him in "A Poet" ("I come to you as a grown child / Who has had a pig-headed father. / I am old enough to make friends.")—just after his first arrival in Europe, in fact—Pound wrote a six-page essay called "What I Think of Walt Whitman." In it he confessed, rather grudgingly, "I see him as America's poet . . ."; he then hastened to add, with characteristic unconsciously comic arrogance, "I honor him because he prophesied me"; after which he went on to assure anyone interested that it was not Whitman's "tricks" (meaning his metrical strategies, his unique diction, tone and voice) that he proposed to make his own, only his "message."

This turns out to be, however, the very reverse of the truth, since Pound in fact tends everywhere to subvert Whitman's "message," his euphoric celebration of democracy and mass society, along with his attack on the traditional High Culture of Europe. But he uses for that purpose (thus simultaneously parodying himself and his model) Whitman's whole bag of "tricks," particularly his metrics: that dactylic or triple falling rhythm, which is characteristic not just of Whitman but of all American as opposed to British speech and provides a viable homegrown alternative to the Old World iambs which Pound prided himself on having broken.

Moreover, Whitman's diction, his odd blend of the adorned rhetorical and the nakedly colloquial provided Pound with a model he desperately needed in order to escape from the archaizing, studiedly quaint poetic diction that blights his earliest poetry: all those "thees" and "thous" and "haths" and "clrisches," which he had learned (twenty years too late, as he himself eventually confessed) from the English Pre-Raphaelites and other exponents of the pseudo-Gothic and the late Victorian "sublime." Some of Pound's first reviewers claimed to detect the influence of Whitman even in his early *fin de siècle* poems; but not until *Riposts* (1912) does he produce a poem which seems to me even remotely Whitmanian. The very title of "N.Y." is a tribute to the first laureate of Manhattan, and the line "Here are a million people surly with traffic" could not have been written without his example. But Pound is still clinging to the cloyingly affected "thou art" and "thou shalt," still afraid to say, like his not quite acknowledged master, simply "you."

He did finally learn to use unabashed that neutral second-person pronoun, which makes impossible discrimination between stranger and familiar, inferior and superior, even singular and plural, in certain uncollected poems like "To Whistler, American," which appeared in 1912, and "Pax Saturni," which appeared a year later. He thus released in himself the true Whitmanian voice and style, complete with incremental repetitions at the beginning of successive lines that not only establish an incantatory cadence but underscore the paradoxes they contain:

> Say there are no oppressions . . .
> Say that labor is pleasant . . .
> Say that I am a traitor . . .

By 1916 he was able to write in *Lustra* (my own favorite collection, perhaps for this reason, of Pound's poetry) verses so close to the Whitmanian model that they seem counterfeits, impersonations, trembling on the verge of parody.

> Go my songs to the lonely and unsatisfied . . .
> Go to the bourgeoise who is dying of her ennuis.
> Go to the women in suburbs,
> Go to the hideously wedded . . .
> Go to those who have delicate lust . . .
> Go out and defy opinion . . .

And the joke implicit in such ambiguous imitations is compounded by the continuing attack in them on their unmistakable model:

> There is no use your quoting Whitman against me,
> His time is not our time, his day and hour were different.

Even in those poems in *Lustra* which do not employ so obviously Whitman's "tricks," Pound found himself able at long last to be comic, irreverent, and downright vulgar, rather than solemn, hightone, and genteel; his posture no longer than that of one too *good* for the America which he had abandoned yet could not cease hectoring and haranguing—but of one who is instead, or at least also—too *bad*. It is therefore fitting (after all,

Whitman had been labeled "the dirtiest beast of the age") that for the first and, I think, the last, the only time in the career of this self-styled rebel, four of his poems intended for Lustra were precensored, discreetly dropped by his timid publisher before the book ever appeared as being—sixty years past the publication date of Leaves of Grass—too blasphemous and/or obscene. In these poems, moreover, and others less obviously offensive ("Study in Aesthetics," for instance, "The Lake Isle," "The Bath Tub," and "The Gypsy"), he was able, thanks once more to Whitman, to write in easy conversational rhythms and an unpretentious demotic diction, so that one is tempted (I, at any rate, am tempted) to think rereading them, hearing them in my inner ear: Here, if anywhere, is the true voice of Ezra Pound, the man of a hundred borrowed voices.

For a long time I was convinced that Pound had no authentic voice of his own at all—only, like a ventriloquist's dummy, pseudo-voices speaking in pseudo-tongues. I am thinking not only of the Mock archaic "British" diction of his earlier poems, his translations from the Provençal and the Italian and, alas, much of The Cantos but also of the counterfeit colloquial "American" dialects, which he uses more rarely in The Cantos, but almost compulsively in his personal letters, early and late, much of his hard-core pornography and especially in his infamous wartime propaganda broadcasts on the Italian radio.

In a letter to a friend about Eliot's possible reaction to the book with which this symposium is centrally concerned, for instance, he writes in execrable Minstrel Show dialect: "And how you gwine to keep Possum in his feedbox when I brings in the Chinas and blackmen? He won't laak for to see no Chinas and blackmen in a bukk about Kulchur." Similarly unconvincing versions of colloquial American (white rather than black) appear also in some of his earliest "light verse." Nor are they confined entirely to poems written for private consumption, like the one included in a letter to his father, sent just after the granting of his M.A., in which he imagines that beleaguered parent complaining, "While you rushed the can / And played the man / Smokin' your fine cheroots, / I had to pay / In a hefty way / for a coon to black your boots." Then speaking for himself, the young poet confesses, "Go little verse, by gumbo, go."

That same psuedo-voice in a similar stage-hick accent is heard in Pound's first published poem as well: a parody of James Whitcomb Riley called "Ezra on the Strike," but with no author's name attached:

> Wal, Thanksgivin' do be comin' round,
> With the price of turkeys on the bound,
> And coal, by gum! that was just found
> Is surely gettin' cheaper.

The title alone is insufficient evidence (fortunately there is other proof) of authorship, since "Ezra" was in the early twentieth century just another disparaging nickname for farmers like "rube" or "hayseed" or "hick." Indeed it is this fact which makes it almost inevitable that one of Pound's favorite parodic voices was, and would remain for as long as he wrote, his version of how subliterate rural Americans talked.

He returns to that voice, at any rate, in the propaganda broadcasts he delivered over the Italian radio during "World War II": those would-be chummy chats in which he tried to persuade his fellow citizens back home that Franklin Delano Roosevelt was stark raving mad and a Jew to boot and that the war into which the "higher kikery" had dragged the unwitting WASPs of England and America was an assault against European culture, civilization itself. That "culture" and "civilization" he conveniently forgot that he himself had described, a war earlier and in a more authentic voice, as "an old bitch gone in the teeth . . . two gross of broken statues . . . a few thousand battered books." Sometimes his language in these broadcasts comes so close to downright travesty of American speech that it is tempting to believe he was only kidding or perhaps deliberately trying to subvert the cause he presumably served, putting one over on Mussolini's intelligence service, which after long soul-searching, had authorized his talks.

But alas, he fooled no one except himself when he said in pseudo-American, "I will teach you kids why you were drugged into the war . . ." or "Democracy has been licked to a frazzle. Property has vamoosed. It has went." If he seems sometimes (not only in these broadcasts but occasionally in *The Cantos* as well, whose paranoic, obsessive compulsive politics and bigotry are indistinguishable from those expressed in his political prose) like a non-native speaker, a double agent from elsewhere trying to pass as an American, he did not know it. Yet sometimes when he was making poems rather than propaganda, his voice is as authentically, unmistakably American as that of Whitman or Mark Twain, Hemingway or Faulkner.

How seldom, though, even in his verse did he find that voice: throughout *Lustra*, as I have already observed, and the first part of *Hugh Selwyn Mauberley* as well; intermittently in *Cathay* and *The Cantos*, particularly the *Pisan Cantos*, where a pain deeper than politics, and a pathos more genuine than self-pity moved him to forsake crankiness and self-parody. It is, in fact, for the sake of this slim remnant of verse that I have accepted your invitation and have slogged once more through the intolerably incoherent and tedious rest of Pound's work, in which his authentic voice is drowned out by a cacophony of counterfeit pseudo-voices in a macaronic echo-chamber, which blur finally into white noise.

The point is that Pound lost faith in the genuine voice he had discovered in 1916 and betrayed it in what is for me an act of treason against himself and against poetry more reprehensible by far than that against his country with which he was legally charged. Yet the former, like the latter, is excusable perhaps on the grounds of "insanity": which is to say, the obsessions (USURA is the root of all evil, Il Duce is our Saviour), the paranoia (the yids are doing us in), and especially the ever-increasing dissociation which afflicted him both in his life and his work. Such dissociation classically manifests itself in the "splitting" of personality, the emergence, once the ego boundaries have been breeched, of multiple quasi-*personae*, speaking in diverse voices for diverse aspects of an intolerably conflicted psyche.

Pound's defenses against such ever-growing dissociation were weapons out of the arsenal of art: the therapeutic acting out of the threatened fragmentation of the self. In his case, this meant, the use, on the one hand, of travesty and burlesque and on the other, of translation and "masking," especially the Dramatic Monologue which he had learned from Robert Browning. Finally, even, his defenses became indistinguishable from his symptoms. The puppets took over from the puppet master— their simulated voices drowning out his own real one. Finally, even parody no longer served to exorcise the alien personae which possessed him. Yet he continued compulsively his life-long practice of travesty and burlesque, taking, for instance, one last parodic smack at Browning late in *The Cantos* ("Oh to be in England now that Winston's out"), which is to say, evoking yet again the Ur-mask he had assumed in order to begin: evoking the poet in whose parodied voice he had originally intended— indeed, had begun—to write all of *The Cantos*.

From the mid-thirties on, in any case, Pound seems to have been at least on the borderline of insanity. It was at that point, for instance, that James Joyce begged Hemingway to accompany him—as a kind of bodyguard—to a dinner *chez* Pound; confessing that he thought him "mad" and was "genuinely frightened of him": an opinion in which Hemingway concurred, observing later that at their meal together Pound had spoken "very erratically." In light of this, it seems somehow fitting that Pound's last published collection of shorter verse, *The Poems of Alfred Venison*, which appeared at that very moment, turned out to be, as its title indicates, hardcore parody: nearly a score of mocking reworkings of the favorite anthology pieces of popular Victorian bards—including not only Tennyson but also Kipling and even Longfellow. Despite the inclusion of that eminent American, however, they were all written in what Pound clearly intended to be Cockney dialect, though it bears about as little resemblance to actual lower-class, urban English speech as the dialect of "Ezra on the Strike" had to genuine rural mid-American.

Between his earliest and latest ventures into parody, moreover, Pound had published similar jocular takeoffs, some wicked, some affectionate, of verse by Byron and Burns, A. E. Housman and Swinburne, as well as the Medieval popular lyric and the poetry of the Irish Renaissance. One of the best of these, his travesty of "Lhude sing Cuckoo," whose irreverent refrain "Lhude sing Goddamn" had led to its being dropped from the first edition of *Lustra*, has since become a standard anthology piece, a part of the Pound canon as taught in our schools. This seems not only a wry joke on changing times and tastes but also a clue to the fact—still generally ignored by critics—that such parody is central to Pound's work.

Indeed (it is an equivocal boast that can be made of no other poet with claims to real distinction, even among parody-prone Americans and Modernists), if all of Pound's work in this intentionally burlesque mode were gathered together, it would make a substantial and not unimpressive volume. It would be even more substantial and impressive if one were to add a selection of some of the many unintentionally hilarious boners which are to be found in his "translations." Robert Graves speaks somewhere of asking his children, who were at home in Mallorcan, a Romance language closely akin to Provençal, what they thought of Pound's approximately English versions of Arnaut Daniel; at which, he tells us, they laughed and laughed and *laughed*. It is a response, I must confess, to which I (who invested a couple of years of my own graduate-student days in the study of poetry in that tongue) am also tempted; as I am, too, rereading Pound's overstuffed, self-indulgent renderings of the slim and austere verses of the Medieval Italian poet Guido Cavalcanti, in which a simple and straightforward phrase like *morte gentil* becomes the pretentiously archaic "death who art haught."

So others—not all of them pedants by any means—have sniggered at his infamous goof in translating the Old English phrase *eorthen rices* in "The Seafarer" as "earthen riches," though of course it means "earthly kingdoms," as well as at his apparent belief in a nonexistent poet called Ri Haku—arising from a failure to realize that this "name" represents only a Japanese reading of the ideograms which spell Li Po.

Such absurdities are risked, of course, not just by translators but by all poets (I think once more of Walt Whitman) who like Pound have the chutzpah to rush in where timid and learned scholars fear to tread. Indeed, I honor him for it; honor him all the more, because I realize, as he clearly did not, that by such travesty he subverts unconsciously the high culture for which he was consciously so solemn, and therefore doubly comic, an apologist—campaigning all his life long, for instance, like some parody schoolmaster, for reinstituting compulsory Latin in America's schools.

In light of all this, you will scarcely be surprised to discover that I think the best way of reading (the only way really to redeem) *The Cantos* themselves is by reading them as unintended—or better perhaps subintended—parody. His *magnum opus*, I am suggesting, is not a failed Epic, though it seemed so to Pound's most sympathetic advocate, T. S. Eliot, and, for that matter, even to him, who when near his death spoke of the long poem at which he had labored for so many years as *sbagliato*, botched, a mistake from the start. It is rather a mock epic, an anti-epic, a comic travesty of the genre, and consequently (as I would dearly love to believe that at some level he suspected) a joke on himself as well as on the latter-day pious Poundolators who do not realize as much. What else are we to make of the passage in Canto 41, in which he approvingly quotes the comments on a sample of his work by Mussolini: "Ma qvesto" / said the boss "è divertente" (the adjective, of course, means "amusing," not to be taken seriously); then he adds, "catching the point / before the aesthetes had got there."

After such a warning, how can "the aesthetes" still read *The Cantos* with a straight face? Had Pound not revealed his not-so-secret parodic intent, even before the fact, as it were, in the title of an early poem, which travesties the famous opening line of the *Aenead*, "Famam Librosque Cano." This warns us clearly enough, does it not, that he sings, will continue to sing, *not* like his Latin model, Arms and the Man, Warfare and the Hero, but Fame and Books, which is to say, making it by producing literature about literature, a scarcely heroic—though diverting—theme.

The Cantos, moreover, not only lack a heroic theme; they lack a heroic protagonist as well. Indeed, they have no proper protagonist at all, not even a parodic one. For a little while, in the earlier Cantos, Odysseus promises to play such a role. He is ironized from the start, however, by the fact that he appears not in a text translated by Homer, but the English version of a Renaissance Latin crib of the original, thrice removed from the original. And even this ghost of a ghost of a ghost soon fades from the scene, or rather, persists only in echoes of the false name Odysseus gave himself as part of his bloody practical joke on the Cyclops. "*Ou tis*" is that name, No Man, Nobody, an appellation nearly anonymous, and therefore fitting for a poet without a proper persona or voice of his own.

What we hear in *The Cantos* is, finally, Nobody talking in garbled and half-understood tongues about a world in which, culture having become Kulchur, nothing matters. Consequently, despite all the references, literary and historical, the allusions and quotations, the dropped names of the living and the dead, the self-annihilating *Cantos* are about Nothing at all.

Only having realized this will the reader be ready to recognize that the real model for *The Cantos* is not Homer's *Odyssey*, much less Vergil's or Dante's pseudo-Homeric Epics, or even

Walt Whitman's *Leaves of Grass*. It is, rather, Flaubert's *Bouvard et Pécuchet*, a thoroughly unreadable work which Pound so extravagantly admired all the same, perhaps because it bears the same parodic relationship to the bourgeois novel as his unfinished, unfinishable poem does to the classic Epic. Flaubert's anti-novel not merely was, but was intended to be, as he warned in announcing it, a book "about nothing." I want to produce, he wrote, "such an impression of lassitude and ennui that as people read the book they will think of its being written by a cretin." Indeed, the same can be said of *The Cantos*, with the substitution perhaps of "madman" for "cretin." Both, at any rate, represent polar, absolute, terminal Parody, parody degree zero, in the sense that no more ultimate parody can be written of either, as I must confess I have tried more than once—producing each time, alas, results less absurd than the original. *Ma questo è divertente.*

8

Where Memory Faileth:
Forgetfulness
and a Poem Including History

Michael North

When Ezra Pound was returned to the United States in 1945, he declared, "I'd die for an idea all right, but to die for an idea I've forgotten is too much. Does anyone have the faintest idea what I said?" The statement is discomforting for a number of different reasons, not the least of which is the claim of poor memory by the poet who had just completed the *Pisan Cantos*. We know that memory loss was one symptom of the breakdown Pound suffered during his term in the gorilla cage, but in between that collapse and his return to the United States, Pound composed ten long cantos that depend on and celebrate the faculty of memory. "Dove sta memoria," the phrase Pound adapts from Cavalcanti, is a kind of motto for these cantos, as it might be for the whole work that begins with a blood offering to the ghosts of the past. And some of Pound's most intemperate outbursts are directed at what he saw as a conspiracy of forgetfulness, a method of writing history "aimed at FORGETTING" the most salient facts. Yet Pound also defined culture as beginning "when one HAS 'forgotten-what-book.'"[1] If culture can be based on forgetting instead of on remembering, then the position of history in a poem like *The Cantos* may be a paradoxical one. The complex strategies by which Pound's poem manages to include history, especially in the later thirties, are directly related to this paradox in his conception of memory.

Pound can hardly be blamed for the fact that the *Pisan Cantos* contain many gaps and lapses of memory, references to "what's his name" (79/486) and "Monsieur Whoosis" (80/511). But such evasions are common in Pound's work before Pisa as well. *Guide to Kulchur* has quite a few references such as the one to "the what's-its-name theatre," and earlier essays such as "Murder by Capital" contain references to historical figures like "what's-his-name, the Elector of Hanover or wherever it was" or to events in "the time of whatever their names were." Contemporary scholars might well envy Pound's courage as he breezes past such empty spots in his knowledge. But at times Pound sounds like the kind of bad lecturer we know all too well who mentions "a Japanese emperor whose name I have forgotten and whose name you needn't remember," apparently because it will not be appearing on the final.[2]

Despite his reverence for memory, Pound consistently shows a disdain for conventional mnemonic accuracy and an impatience with minute facts, the citation of which might impede his rhetorical progress. More than impatience is involved, however, in other, more complex lapses of memory. In his review of Laurence Binyon's translation of the *Inferno*, Pound laments that the "younger generation may have forgotten Binyon's sad youth." Aside from the fact that only the older generation can have had the opportunity to forget Binyon's youth, it soon turns out that Pound himself has forgotten it: "Demme if I remember anything but a word." Pound was prone to such odd self-contradictions also in the radio speeches, which contain a number of queerly self-destructive passages like this one: "After Winston's visit to Washington, have you mental coherence enough to recall what happened in England when the fat boy brought back the gold standard? Must have been YEARS ago, did someone say 1925? I have plumb forgot when it happened."³ That Pound should castigate his listeners for the incoherence of their memories, while displaying a far greater incoherence in his own, may be the sort of contradiction allowed to great polemicists. On the other hand, such contradictions suggest that memory is not a simple matter for Pound, not purely the reverential faculty that it appears in the *Pisan Cantos.*

From the very beginning of his career, Pound derided mechanical memory. In 1914, he declared that "his respect for the mnemonic mind has been lessened by contact." Some twenty years later, *Guide to Kulchur* begins with Kung's declaration that he does not depend on memory. These comments can be harmonized with Pound's obvious reverence for memory by identifying two different kinds of memory, each appropriate to a different kind of knowledge. As Pound says, "It does not matter a two-penny damn whether you load up your memory with the chronological sequence of what has happened, or the names of protagonists, or authors of books, or generals and leading political spouters, so long as you understand the process now going on." There is a basic difference between rote memorization of such facts and knowledge of processes, knowledge which is "weightless, held without effort."⁴

Elsewhere in *Guide to Kulchur* Pound draws a distinction between knowledge that must be looked up and committed to memory and that which is "part of my total disposition." The distinction is between effortful memorization and natural, effortless memory, and though it does determine both the form and subject of *Guide to Kulchur,* the distinction itself depends in a paradoxical way on the opposite faculty of forgetfulness. For the more important kind of knowledge, held in the more authentic memory, is simply that which resists forgetfulness: "I am to put down so far as possible only what has resisted the erosion of time, and forgetfulness." If forgetfulness is a threat, it is also a kind of test, because knowledge that must be constantly maintained is simply not part of that "total disposition"

which is the source of true memory. *Guide to Kulchur* is formed
by Pound's belief in this test. Pound freely admits that "I cd. by
opening volumes I haven't seen for 25 or more years find data
that run counter to what I am saying." But such volumes are
unimportant precisely because they must be looked up. When
Pound says, "In the main, I am to write this new Vade Mecum
without opening other volumes," he is announcing that the
book is a kind of stunt, a test of his own memory but also of
what he has read, which is to be judged by the way it withstands
Pound's forgetfulness. A few pages into the *Guide*, Pound allows
that, contrary to what he has just been saying, Aristotle may
have made some worthy suggestions about conduct. But "I
don't remember 'em at the moment. Any more than I remember Plato's having thought about money, which lapse may
mean that thirty years ago neither I nor anyone else read Plato
. . . with an enlightened economic curiosity."5

Notice that this lapse of memory becomes the occasion for a
judgment, first of the forgotten source, then of Pound himself,
and finally of the society at large. There is no attempt to discuss
Plato's views on money, because the issue here is the knowledge available to the writer of the *Guide* at the moment of its
conception. Pound takes this regimen to extraordinary lengths.
He admits in a footnote to an early criticism of Aristotle that he
had forgotten the beginning of his own book by the time he
neared the end. This lapse is trivial, however, because it turns
out that Pound has used exactly the same terms to describe
Aristotle in both cases: "I leave these repetitions so that the
strict reader can measure the difference, if any, between this
'residuum' left in my memory or whatever, and the justification
or unjustification given in detail later."6 What might have been
seen as an extraordinary lapse of attention becomes a valida-
tion of his method and his memory. To be sure, Pound does
refer at times to other books, despite his vow. For example, he
takes down Bacon from the shelf. It then turns out that he has
read Bacon, though he has forgotten having done so, but it

does not matter because Bacon uncannily agrees with Pound's estimation of Aristotle. Thus the system is validated again, because what is crucially useful in the source has remained with Pound, though he has lost even the knowledge of having read the book.

In the writing of *Guide to Kulchur,* the resistance of the memory becomes a test of the value of knowledge, not so much a qualitative test as a kind of discrimination between mere facts and details that can become part of the "process" valued as true knowledge. Similarly, the strength of a writer's resistance to new material can be an index of the completeness of his memory. Pound once said of James that "the actual mechanism of his scriptorial processes became so bulky, became so huge a contrivance for record and depiction, that the old man simply couldn't remember or keep his mind on or animadvert on anything but the authenticity of his impression."[7] This comment is not so much a description of James as an eerie look into Pound's own future. The inability to remember here marks for Pound not the partiality but the completeness and the authenticity of the writer's knowledge. In writing *Guide to Kulchur,* Pound attempts to become this kind of writer, with this kind of authenticity protected by forgetfulness.

If such an emphasis on the power of forgetfulness seems to turn the concept of memory inside out, a look at one poem can help to verify that this inversion is Pound's own. The first issue of *Blast* contains a poem entitled "Monumentum Aere, etc." The "etc." is a rather engaging gesture, since the title is a fragment of Horace's famous claim for the durability of verse. The abbreviation thus becomes a backhanded tribute to Horace, a shrug toward the audience as if to say, "But you know the rest." The poem itself has a paradoxical relationship to Horace's ode because it emphasizes not memory but forgetfulness, not the durability of verse but a convenient impermanence in it:

You say that I take a good deal upon myself;
That I strut in the robes of assumption.

In a few years no one will remember the "buffo,"
No one will remember the trivial parts of me,
The comic detail will not be present.
As for you, you will lie in the earth,
And it is doubtful if even your manure will be rich enough

To keep grass
Over your grave.[8]

The poem certainly intends to claim, at least implicitly, that the poet will outlast his detractors. But much unlike Horace, Pound emphasizes the way time will preserve his work by eliminating the trivial from it; there is no overt mention of memory or permanence in the poem at all. In fact, the poem describes exactly the process identified in the James essay, whereby time perfects the poet by allowing him to forget. The "etc." of the title then comes to represent not what is remembered by all but what is forgotten, and Pound's title represents rather tersely the way he inverts Horace by only partially preserving him.

In a strange way, then, forgetfulness assumes the role conventionally assigned to memory. In *Guide to Kulchur* this reversal is at first personal, as Pound comes to resemble the James he describes in the earlier essay, and then it is cultural. In one instance, Pound turns his own poor memory into a new paradigm for culture. Groping for a quotation, he says, "Ford has mentioned it in a book that a human being can read. I have forgotten what book." Then he calls the audience to order with a boldface subhead and announces, "Knowledge is NOT culture. The domain of culture begins when one HAS 'forgotten-what-book.'" Though he is at first clearly attempting to justify what has been his method of composition from the beginning of *Guide to Kulchur,* Pound allows his outrageous and seemingly uncharacteristic statement to become a new definition of culture. The definition is illustrated by the opposition drawn between Boccherini and Bartok, in which Boccherini represents culture and Bartok the kind of struggle undergone by individuals such as Beethoven and Pound himself when culture ceases to be an unconscious possession. As Donald Davie points out, the two antithetical composers correspond to the two different kinds of knowledge described earlier in the book: "The knowledge that one possesses securely is not safe-guarded consciously, nor even is it so acquired; it is like a trained reflex, not maintained or extended by any act of will."[9] Extended to culture, this dichotomy separates the conscious, contrived culture of modern times and an unconscious, sec-ond-nature kind of culture that does not depend on libraries or retrieval systems. Pound apparently wants to say here that there are two kinds of memory, rote and traditional, and that true culture exists where rote memory is unnecessary because all the crucial knowledge of the clan is possessed naturally by its members. But his outburst about books is revealing, and it reveals more than what Pound admits immediately thereafter, that he does not belong to such a traditional culture himself.

In an essay entitled "Eliot and a Common Culture," Terry Eagleton points out the way in which Eliot habitually hovers between two rather different definitions of the word *culture*: "roughly, the arts on one hand and a way of life on the other." One definition is that which can be associated with Arnold, the other that made more common by modern anthropology. Eliot, in fact, begins the early, periodical version of *Notes towards a Definition of Culture* by insisting on this very distinction, which becomes in the final version the key distinction between "culture" and "a culture." The first is the conscious achievement of an elite, while the second is the common possession of a whole people. Eagleton admits that Eliot is conscious of using the word in both senses, as when he speaks of "the hereditary transmission of culture within a culture."[10] But Eagleton is concerned to point out the trouble that can come from a con-fusion of the two definitions, especially of assuming too easily that literature and the arts are identical to the customs, habits, and beliefs anthropologists call "culture." In his separation of

Boccherini and Bartok, Pound seems not to be using two different definitions but to be defining culture against its opposite. But the contrast is in fact between two different kinds of
culture that correspond to the two different kinds of knowledge
described earlier: one kind of culture is an unconscious possession; the other, the result of conscious preservation and
transmission. Like Eliot, Pound hovers between these two definitions, and the role of forgetfulness is to help to bridge the
gap between them.

Pound has an easy pejorative always to hand in the German
word *Kultur,* a word that is originally Poundian shorthand for
the German philological tradition. Pound uses the word to
encompass state education, rote learning, and academic log-
rolling. His lifelong use of the term in this way prompts the
search for another term, ultimately found in Frobenius. "Frobenius escaped both the fiddling term 'culture' and rigid 'Kultur' by
recourse to Greek, he used 'Paideuma' [which] means the mental formation, the inherited habits of thought, the con-
ditionings, aptitudes of a given race or time."[11] The change in
terminology helps to differentiate between culture as an im-
position and as an unconscious possession. *Kultur* is the re-
gimentation of the best; paideuma, the aggregation of the
whole.

The distinction is still in Pound's mind as he contemplates
the method of *Guide to Kulchur.* At the beginning of that volume
he recalls the British Museum reading room and his calcula-
tions of how long it would take to encompass all that material
by study. Like many students and professors since, he felt that
"there must be some other way for a human being to make use
of that vast cultural heritage," and that other way became apparent in Frobenius: "He has in especial seen and marked out a
kind of knowing, the difference between knowledge that has to
be acquired by particular effort and knowing that is in people,
'in the air.'"[12] *Guide to Kulchur* rests on this distinction, which
appears when Pound differentiates between Boccherini and

Bartok. But it should be made apparent that the definition of culture has shifted. Frobenius does not promise access to the culture of the British Museum reading room. His paideuma is the anthropologist's culture, not that which is contained in literature and the arts. It is crucial, however, for Pound to insist that some version of the reading to be had in that room exists "in the air," and he does so against the very implications of Frobenius. For the really crucial limitation of the paideuma is that it cannot be learned at all. Unlike *Kultur*, which at least is a methodology that can be practiced by anyone, the paideuma, since it is transmitted by inheritance, is a closed book to those outside and, what is perhaps more ominous for Pound, inseparable from the social, political, and geographic conditions in which it exists.

There can be no guide to such a culture, which Pound admits by placing himself with Bartok instead of Boccherini. But throughout *Guide to Kulchur* and Pound's poetry of this period, there are constant implications to the contrary. One such implication is contained in the close identification Pound sees between the anthropological observer and the culture under observation. The most common, indeed almost the sole, example of paideuma in *Guide to Kulchur* is the unearthing of "the bronze car of Dis" in a railway cutting, where peasants had opposed the excavation. The peasant's traditional, collective knowledge of what lies underground resembles the archaeologist's in a way, and in fact Frobenius himself could say, "If you will go to a certain place and there digge, you will find traces of a civilization." So close is the resemblance between these two talents that, two hundred pages farther into the *Guide*, Pound makes the peasant's discovery into Frobenius's: "That a man find the car of Persephone in a German burrow is already a mental property."[13] By transposing race memory into a personal quality, Pound is able to imply that the culture of the peasants can be acquired by outsiders.

The peculiar role of forgetfulness in this transposition may now be described. Although Pound identifies Boccherini with a culture that begins "when one HAS 'forgotten-what-book,'" this view cannot define culture as lived and experienced by Boccherini himself, simply because he had nothing to forget, just as he had nothing consciously to learn. For him, culture was truly "in the air," and just this ease of possession marks him off from a later composer such as Bartok. Forgetfulness enters only if Bartok tries to become like Boccherini, lacking the hereditary transmission of his time and place. To become like Boccherini, Pound must somehow both learn and forget. He must first possess the book and then forget having done so. Forgetfulness therefore comes into play when a culture that is consciously acquired and maintained is to be transformed into an unconscious one. What is effaced, of course, is not the knowledge itself but the unpleasant fact of having had to learn it.

The mental and stylistic gyrations necessitated by this transformation are visible in another passage on Frobenius. "Frobenius forgets his note book, ten miles from camp he remembers it. Special African feast on, and no means of sketching it for the records. No time to return to camp. No matter. Black starts drumming. Drum telegraph works and sketching materials arrive in time for the beano." The anecdote itself is complex enough, but Pound's summary comment "culture possessed and forgotten" complicates it further. The context seems to make it clear that it is the Africans who have possessed their culture in such a thorough way that they can communicate over long distances. But what, precisely, can they have forgotten? Frobenius has forgotten something—his notebook, which is the symbol of the sort of artificial memory he needs in order to participate in this culture. Rather than illustrating the possible benefits to a modern European society of the kind of culture Frobenius studies, the anecdote vividly illustrates the radical difference between the two. Yet "culture possessed and forgotten" is Pound's description of what poets like himself must do.

Culture, he says, is "what is left after a man has forgotten all he sets out to learn." Or, as he says in the essay on Cavalcanti, "It takes six or eight years to get educated in one's art, and another ten to get rid of that education."[14] In the anecdote, African cultural memory saves Frobenius where his own notebook memory fails, but the scientist can only truly resemble his subjects when he commits again the act of forgetfulness, deliberately casting the notebook aside.

Frobenius is such a hero to Pound partly because he seems to combine two different kinds of culture, only one of which is actually available to modern Europeans like Pound, Frobenius, and Bartok. Through study, the anthropologist comes to resemble his subjects, who sustain their culture without study or other effort. But Pound wants to go far beyond Frobenius, beyond mere study, to write a poem that will both demonstrate and proselytize for the new paideuma. The didactic method of Pound's literary project further complicates the already paradoxical situation described in *Guide to Kulchur.* As a polemicist for the new paideuma, Pound must preach from outside the promised land, standing, as he realizes he does, on the same dubious ground as Bartok, outside of *any* organized culture. As a teacher, Pound must attempt to re-create consciously what should ideally be an unconscious, natural possession, transmitted without teaching and in fact unteachable. These paradoxes help to explain, I think, some of the difficulties that beset Pound's poetry in the later thirties, when his various definitions of culture come to their sharpest collision.

The recurrent praise of forgetfulness in Pound's prose of this period calls into question his definition of the epic as a poem including history. Though *The Cantos* certainly include what we conventionally recognize as history, the actual value of history in the synthetic culture postulated by the poem is unclear. If, as Pound suggests in Canto 86, there is in nature a kind of culture "needing no verbal tradition" (86/573), perhaps history as a study is not really necessary. Pound's own view of civilization often seems ahistorical, as Michael André Bernstein suggests, in that the movement of humanity through time is not really a progression or a regression but a series of variations around a single invariable standard.[15] That Pound in Canto 76 can celebrate the correspondence, over centuries, of Shun's will and King Wan's will, the "two halves of a tally stick," suggests that for him the most perfect civilization existed almost at the beginning of time and that all variation from its static perfection means demise. Of course, *The Cantos* contain more than one kind of history and many different ideas about the histories contained in it, but the more overtly historical of *The Cantos*, the China cantos, 52–61, put history in the most equivocal position.

The China cantos, among Pound's most didactic, are also the densest and most confusing. It is particularly discouraging, especially to the diligent reader who has faithfully struggled through ten long cantos of what seems a lot like history, to read at the very end that "Chiyeou didn't do it on book readin' / nor by mugging up history" (61/338). De Mailla tells us that the farmer Shih-yu was praised by the emperor Yung-cheng in an eighteenth-century edict for returning a lost bag of silver and thus demonstrating reverence toward the innate sense of justice in all people.[16] Pound's own faith in such justice can be bracing, but it is also demoralizing to the reader to be told that reading is unnecessary and to have nearly a hundred pages of history close with a dismissal of history. One way to read these lines, however, is as a rather brutal exposure of the difference between Shih-yu and ourselves, dependent, in our latter day, on artificial virtue. Whether we can ever approximate the virtue of Shih-yu is unknown, but if we must approach that virtue by reading books, even Pound's, we will apparently be eternally distant from it.

What then is the purpose of the history in the China cantos? This question might be answered by observing how history, as a study of the past, is treated by the figures described in the poem. In Canto 54, the emperor Kao Ti, as one of his several acts of exemplary virtue, restores "the books," the Shu Ching and the Shih Ching (54/276). These books are, in fact, exactly the ones Shih-yu did not read,[17] but at this period of history they seem necessary and the emperor rules wisely in restoring them. The books need restoring because about eleven years earlier they had been burned by order of the emperor Chi Hoang Ti, who *also* receives Pound's approbation:

> and after 33 years burnt the books
> > because of fool litterati
> by counsel of Li-ssé
> > save medicine and on field works.
> > > (54/275)

Though this step was in fact a political move against Confucianism as much as anything,[18] I think we must see it as one of those periodic rectifications necessary to keep learning and virtue in good order. As the example of Shih-yu shows, in any case, true Confucian virtue can remain in the absence of the history classics, though apparently excessive concentration on them can obscure the real core of Confucianism. Thus Pound says in Canto 76,

> better gift can no man make to a nation
> than the sense of Kung fu Tseu
> . . . .
> nor in historiography nor in making anthologies.
> > (76/454)

History, or learning about the past from books, is unnecessary as long as the "sense" of Confucius is preserved. And this "sense" is not so much a set of rules and procedures as it is the whole context of China, that which makes the culture what it is ("Kung is to China as is water to fishes" [54/285]). We should notice in reading these cantos that even those great rulers who preserve and respect the Confucian classics do not become great through the classics. History may at times be for Pound a schoolbook for princes, but these cantos do not show emperors achieving greatness by reading the classic works. Rather the good emperors demonstrate their greatness by reverence toward the works as symbols. The emperor's success comes from knowing how to swim in the water that is China; no more than a whale does he need a book to tell him how to do it. If he does happen to feel reverence for the books, it is only because they are a convenient representation of the path he has already followed, and if excessive study should conflict with or obscure the true way, he is quite justified in destroying the books.

How does this equivocal attitude toward history books affect the writing of history in *The Cantos*? First of all, it should call into question the initial assumption that these are didactic poems, since they demonstrate that literary didacticism is, at the very least, beside the point. Pound was certainly convinced that many Confucian principles are transferable, and therefore transmittable, but in the poem such transmission is effected not by books but by the basic conditions of life in China. Non-Confucian leaders bring about poverty, disease, unrest, and ultimately their own downfall, while Confucian leaders bring about a stabilizing harmony. To return to Pound's metaphor, at times the fish try to swim out of the water, but inevitably they must return to their proper medium. The metaphor helps to explain as well the pattern of history described in these cantos. The China cantos do not represent struggles between individuals, organizations, or ideas, but a pattern of deviation from and return to one standard of truth. As Bernstein puts it, Confucian historiography sees the field of history as "a closed arena," with eternal repetitions governed by the same fixed rules.[19]

The history contained in such works is ultimately tautological, a history composed of self-evident definitions. For when the ruler ceases to act by the precepts of Confucius, he simply ceases to be a ruler, both by definition and finally in fact. As Peter Nicholls has recently explained, relying on Levenson and Schurmann's history of China, "A king does not starve or slaughter his people, because it is of the essence of kingship that a king brings harmony to the realm. If one fails in this and is yet called a king then that name must be rectified."[20] Written history, following such a belief, describes essences instead of acts, and it is by nature circular and repetitive, since the king who is not kingly ceases to be king, succeeded in the mandate by a truly kingly king. Much of the reaction of the common reader to the China cantos comes, I think, not from their obscurity or even their length per se but from the unimpeachable closure of Pound's system. All conclusions are foregone in such a history; all action, nothing but the acknowledgment of the obvious.

This kind of historiography seems to leave very little room for the reader. It is difficult to disagree with a tautology, but it is also superfluous to accede. Since this sort of history is meant not to teach or convince but simply to acknowledge the obvious, the reader's role must be something like that of the Chinese emperors themselves in their use of the Confucian histories. Either reverence or impiety is the possible reaction, not agreement or disagreement, comprehension or incomprehension. Perhaps the most revealing such use of history comes in Canto 61, when the people receive

> the volumes of history
> with a pee-rade with portable cases like tabernacles
> the dynastic history with solemnity.
> (6/336)

Here the history book is worshiped as an artifact, with a reverence toward history as such, not as conveyer of anything.

Another role Pound has in mind for his readers is revealed in an odd way toward the end of the section in Canto 60. For one of the few times in the China cantos, Europeans appear on the scene, exposing themselves as Europeans by their superfluous and foolish questions.

having heard that the Chinese rites honour Kung-fu-tseu
and offer sacrifice to the Heaven etc/
and that their ceremonies are grounded in reason
now beg to know their true meaning and in particular
the meaning of terms for example Material
Heaven and Changti meaning? its ruler?
Does the *manes* of Confucius
accept the grain, fruit, silk, incense offered
                  and does he enter his cartouche?
The European church wallahs wonder if this can be reconciled.
                                                    (60/330)

With some of his old wit, Pound skewers the European
churchmen on their own silly controversies, the absurdity of
which is exposed by the transposition into Confucian terms.
But Pound has not told his readers enough to make these
questions seem utterly superfluous, and many readers may
find themselves waiting for the answers that never come. If so,
they have failed a kind of test or missed an opportunity offered
by the poem, because the true oddity of this section of Canto
60 is that it coolly invites us to see the Europeans as ignorant
outsiders, as if we were Confucian mandarins in the highest
degree. Of course, most of us are ignorant Europeans, and the
chance to see ourselves for a moment reveals the essential
strategy of these poems, which is to place us from the first
inside the Confucian system as if it were our own ancestral
heritage. Only by accepting this position can we manage to
fulfill our role in these histories, which is to take them for
granted. Only by giving us such a role can the poem succeed in
its basic task, which is to give the Confucian system an inev-
itability beyond all question. The China cantos make history
not into a story for us to read but into water in which we either
sink or swim.

Pound ends the China cantos, however, on a slightly different
note. Canto 61 ends in praise of the Ch'ien-lung emperor who
lowered taxes and condensed histories and wrote some

poems. The final line of these ten long cantos addresses the reader directly: "Perhaps you will look up his verses" (61/340). In irony, this line is worthy of Pound's homage to Propertius. The "perhaps" carries just the right weight of skepticism. The line does not in fact advise us to look up those verses; it surrounds the act of looking up with an irony so devilish that readers are wrong no matter what they do. We are here only two pages from the story of Shih-yu, who "didn't do it on book readin'," and, of course, the whole thrust of these cantos has been to render book readin' superfluous, if not suspect. The line also bears an ironic relationship to the distinctions worked out in *Guide to Kulchur*, where the knowledge that must be looked up is dismissed.

Davie suggests that the first cantos devoted to John Adams, the early Nuevo Mundo cantos, are meant "to do no more than tease the reader into looking up [Pound's] source," which might explain as well the taunt that ends Canto 61. At least one wartime radio speech uses unidentified material solely to goad the audience into realizing its own ignorance.[21] When Pound claims in Canto 67 that "the materials are at the service of the public" (67/387), he seems to be admitting that this section of his poem is meant to send us to its voluminous sources. But these insinuations remain an embarrassment in the poem because they betray Pound's own uneasiness about his project. The irony and ambiguity of the final line of the China cantos betray Pound's own skepticism about his ability to work positively toward a renewed culture. As Eliot puts it, one cannot build a tree; nor can Pound build up through literature what requires the cooperation of race, time, and geography. If one cannot build a tree, one can, to switch from Eliot's metaphor to Pound's, at least clear the underbrush away from it—and this possibility presents forgetfulness in yet another role.

Pound's teaching was always as much negative as positive, pruning and eliminating as well as building up. With *Guide to Kulchur*, though, a different emphasis appears. At the very be-

ginning of the book, Kung accompanies his dismissal of mere
memory by announcing that his own system is a condensation:
"I have reduced it all to one principle." The distinction between
sheer memory and a unitary knowledge achieved through condensation runs throughout the book. Pound draws a distinction in himself between memorized facts and knowledge that is
part of his "total disposition," and he speaks of the possibility
of "taking a totalitarian hold on our history." He is suggesting
here that whole countries can accomplish what he and Confucius have accomplished, reducing their dependence on rote
memory by integrating knowledge into a single, unitary, and
total form. To take this totalitarian hold on history is to grasp
the truly permanent nature of a country, which is inscribed in
its "blood and bone," integrating all its activities into a kind of
group personality.[22]

Elsewhere, Pound defines this group personality and associ-
ates it with the kind of folk culture studied by Frobenius. Curi-
ously, he sees the culture of the folk or the masses as arrived at
by selection. "The blessing of the 'folk' song is solely in that the
'folk' forget and leave out things. It is a fading and attrition not a
creative process." In "Murder by Capital" Pound says that the
mass culture "sifts out and consigns to the ash-can a great deal
that the generation of accepted authors of Mr. Arnold Bennett's
period put in." Thus a people achieves its culture primarily by
negation, by forgetting what does not make a place for itself in
the national paideuma. The optimum kind of culture therefore
is unitary and simple. In the essay "National Culture," he asserts that a "national culture has a minimum of components."
But these few components do not exist in contradistinction to
other, noncultural materials. What remains outside the total
culture is not set aside or subordinated but quite literally forgotten. Only in this way does the exclusive culture acquire the
totality so important to Pound at this time. That this totality is
perilously close to the totalitarian becomes clear when Mussolini is praised for "all he has sloughed off in evolving his

totalitarian formulae."[23] Like Confucius, Mussolini removes superfluities from his mind, forgetting so as to remember. Ominously, Mussolini's ability to ignore what does not fit his "totalitarian formulae" becomes a model of the whole cultural process.

The concept of totality is pertinent to, and entirely benign in its relationship to, Frobenius's view of culture because that view is inclusive. By definition, the anthropological purview includes everything that a culture is and does. In Pound's sense, however, totality is the result of a process of selection, a combination that overlays Arnold's idea of culture on Frobenius's. The problem occurs not with the good that is selected but with the bad that is rejected, a category that simply does not exist for the anthropologist. To retain its totality, Pound's mythical culture cannot simply choose some options and decline others, because the nature of totality rests on the fact that there is no residuum, nothing outside the system. What is not selected must therefore be destroyed, expunged, forgotten, and we all must be aware, with some sadness and I suppose some amusement, that Pound accepted this task with relish.

But it is a task that, by its very nature, cannot be accomplished. In the James essay, Pound says that "most good prose arises, perhaps, from an instinct of negation; is the detailed, convincing analysis of something detestable; of something which one wants to eliminate." Though Pound defines poetry here as quite the opposite, *The Cantos* very often exhibit the same urge to destroy. This urge is, as Pound himself realizes, bound to frustrate itself: "It is also contendable that one must depict such mush in order to abolish it." Much of the ferocity of Pound's rhetoric comes, I think, from the knowledge of being trapped in this contradiction, of being forced to depict what ought to be forgotten. The metaphors that Pound uses for what he disapproves of, the cloacal and bacterial metaphors primarily, mark it as that which must be expelled. But of course, rhetoric can never de-create anything; it makes by naming, and the longer it denounces what it wishes to expel, the longer that horrid substance holds the stage. In a letter to Felix Schelling, Pound says, "There are things I quite definitely want to destroy, and which I think will have to [be] annihilated before civilization can exist. . . . Until the cells of humanity recognize certain things as excrement, they will stay in [the] human colon and poison it." All of Pound's diatribes are against excrement, a metaphor that is chosen not to identify but to annihilate the superfluous. But as Pound himself realizes, "All violence is useless (even the violence of language)."[24]

Pound's willingness to ignore this realization involves him, and us, in several difficulties. Pound's distaste for what he hates increases as he is forced to talk about it, and the rhetoric builds upon itself as he attempts to do the impossible, to destroy with words. The vagueness of much of Pound's polemic may come from a reluctance to elaborate on what he does not want to mention at all. The greatest difficulty, however, confronts Pound in his role as teacher. If Confucius and Mussolini reach a "total disposition" by sloughing off superfluities, and if folk cultures do so naturally, how are his readers to follow? Is it possible for a modern culture to forget what has made it in order to reachieve the unity and totality of the past? In other words, can there be a history that works backward? Though most of us find it easy to forget by accident, it is psychologically nearly impossible to forget something on purpose. If one attempts to do so, one is likely to find that the material to be forgotten overwhelms instead what one wants to remember, which I suggest is just what happens in Pound's work of the early forties. Instead of disappearing as they should, the usurers and those innocent scapegoats, the Jews, become the true gods of Pound's universe.

One of the very earliest histories (if it can be so called), Hesiod's *Theogony*, puts its own status in question by a contradictory approach to memory. Hesiod tells us first that the muses are daughters of Mnemosyne, and yet he also tells us that the purpose of the muses is to help people forget. Perhaps the function of fanciful genealogies is to help people forget, and the purpose of history may be to obscure the truly unpleasant ways in which events actually come to bear on our lives. Nietzsche certainly felt that action needed to wrestle itself free of history and could do so only by a kind of studious forgetfulness, a dominance achieved somehow, by some faculty, over our own memories. What brought Nietzsche to this pass is the fearful apprehension that what we now possess is not culture, not even a debased culture, but "knowledge about culture."[25] How can this "knowledge about" be transformed back into its original subject matter? Can a reflective literature ever transcend reflectiveness so as to reassume the primary status of action itself? The deformations and difficulties of Pound's work of the thirties and forties can be traced, I think, to a tremendous effort to answer these questions.

Notes

Nature and Design (Harriet Zinnes)

1. Ezra Pound, A Memoir of Gaudier-Brzeska (New York: New Directions, 1970), p. 44.

2. Nancy Cox-McCormack, "Memoirs of Conversations with the American Poet, Ezra Pound, and His Wife, Dorothy Shakespear Pound, in Europe, 1921–1931" (Cornell University, Olin Research Library, Rare Books Department).

3. Ford Madox Ford, Outlook, July 31, 1915; Ezra Pound, Ezra Pound and the Visual Arts, ed. Harriet Zinnes (New York: New Directions, 1980), p. 249.

4. Ezra Pound, "The Garden," in Selected Poems (New York: New Directions, 1957), p. 26; Pound, Visual Arts, p. 261.

5. Pound, Memoir, pp. 49, 45.

6. Ibid., pp. 47–48.

7. Ibid., pp. 48, 145.

8. Richard Cork, Henri Gaudier and Ezra Pound, a Friendship (London: A. d'Offay, 1982), p. 11. See also by the same author, Vorticism and Abstract Art in the First Machine Age, 2 vols. (Berkeley and Los Angeles: University of California Press, 1976).

9. Cork, Gaudier and Pound, p. 11. On March 10, 1914, Pound wrote to Dorothy Shakespear, "Brzx's [Brzeska's] column gets more gravely beautiful and phallic each week." And then the poet adds, stressing

the Head's Vorticist intent, "I think it will have a deal of energy as a composition of masses" (Ezra Pound, *Ezra Pound and Dorothy Shakespear: Their Letters, 1909–1914*, ed. Omar Pound and A. Walton Litz [New York: New Directions, 1984], p. 323; see also pp. 273n, 317n).

10. Timothy Materer, *Vortex Pound, Eliot, and Lewis* (Ithaca: Cornell University Press, 1979), p. 94; Pound, *Memoir,* p. 50.

11. Pound, *Memoir,* p. 50.

12. A Marinetti work entitled *Viva la France* (1914, brush and ink, crayon, cut-and-pasted papers, 12⅛″ × 12¾″), with the works of the title *Zang Tumb Tuum* playfully arranged, is in the permanent collection of the Museum of Modern Art.

13. Cork, *Vorticism* 1:63.

14. Pound, *Visual Arts,* p. 13.

15. Pound, *Memoir,* p. 20.

16. Cork, *Vorticism* 1:25.

17. Wyndham Lewis, *Wyndham Lewis on Art,* ed. Walter Michel and C. J. Fox (New York: Funk and Wagnalls, 1969), p. 96.

18. *Blast No.* 2, July 1915, p. 40; Cork, *Vorticism* 1:283; Materer, *Vortex Pound,* p. 119; *Blast No.* 2, p. 45.

19. Pound, *Memoir,* pp. 26, 92; Cork, *Vorticism* 1:282; Pound, *Visual Arts,* p. 183.

20. Pound, *Memoir,* p. 24; Reed Way Dasenbrock, "Vorticism among the Isms," in *Blast 3,* ed. Seamus Cooney (Santa Barbara, Calif.: Black Sparrow Press, 1984), pp. 42–44.

21. Lewis, *Rude Assignment: A Narrative of My Career Up-to-Date* (London: Hutchinson, 1950), p. 129.

22. Douglas Goldring, *South Lodge: Reminiscences of Violet Hunt, Ford Madox Ford, and the English Review Circle, 1943* (London: Constable, 1943), p. 68; Pound, *Memoir,* p. 31.

23. Guy Davenport, *The Geography of the Imagination: Forty Essays* (San Francisco: North Point Press, 1981), p. 158.

Pound's Economics (James Laughlin)

1. References are to *The Cantos* (New York: New Directions, 1972). Quotations are identified by the number of the canto and the number of the page, the two numbers separated by a slash.

2. *Pavannes and Divagations* (New York: New Directions, 1958). Quotations from the shorter poems are from *Personae* (New York: New Directions, 1971).

Pound's Cantos and Confucianism (Chang Yao-hsin)

1. Eliot, *Collected Poems, 1909–1962* (New York: Harcourt, Brace and World, 1963), pp. 29, 53; French, "The Age of Eliot: The Twenties as Wasteland," in *The Twenties: Fiction, Poetry, Drama,* ed. Warren French (Deland, Fla.: Everett/Edwards, 1975), p. 4; Yeats, "The Second Coming," in *The Collected Poems of W. B. Yeats* (New York: Macmillan, 1960), p. 185; Pound, *Patria mia* (Chicago: Seymour, 1950), p. 41; Pound, "Henry James and Remy de Gourmount," in *Make It New: Essays by Ezra Pound* (New Haven: Yale University Press, 1935), p. 253; Frohock, "The Revolt of Ezra Pound," in *Ezra Pound: A Collection of Critical Essays,* ed. Walter Sutton (Englewood Cliffs, N.J.: Prentice-Hall, 1963), p. 91.

2. For the Krutch and Russell citations, see F. J. Hoffman, *The Twenties: American Writing in the Post-War Decade* (New York: Free Press, 1949), pp. 276–77. References to Pound are in *Selected Prose, 1909–1965,* ed. William Cookson (New York: New Directions, 1973), p. 77; *The Letters of Ezra Pound, 1907–1941,* ed. D. D. Paige (New York: Harcourt, Brace, 1950), p. 183; *Little Review Anthology,* ed. Margaret C. Anderson (New York: Horizon Press, 1970), p. 100; *Letters,* p. 345; *The Cantos* (New York: New Directions, 1972), Canto 61, p. 334. References to this edition of *The Cantos* will give canto number and page number, separated by a slash.

3. Ezra Pound, *Guide to Kulchur* (Norfolk, Conn.: New Directions, 1952), pp. 23–24, 219, 306.

4. Pound, *Selected Prose,* p. 79; Pound, *Letters,* p. 217.

5. Pound, *Selected Prose,* p. 76; Kenner, *The Poetry of Ezra Pound* (Norfolk, Conn.: New Directions, 1968), p. 50; Jung, "Ezra Pound and China" (Ph.D diss., University of Washington, 1955), p. 96.

6. Massimo Bacigalupo, *The Formed Trace: Later Poetry of Ezra Pound* (New York: Columbia University Press, 1980), p. 185.

7. Confucius, *The Great Digest, the Unwobbling Pivot, the Analects,* tr. Ezra Pound (Norfolk, Conn.: New Directions, 1928), p. 22.

8. I have followed Amy Lowell's version of the poem, in *Fir-Flower Tablets* (Boston: Houghton Mifflin, 1921), p. 27.

9. Jung, "China," p. 109.

10. "The Confucian Analects," in *The Four Books: The Confucian Analects, the Great Learning, the Doctrine of the Mean, and the Works of Mencius*, tr. James Legge (Shanghai: Chinese Book Company, n.d.), p. 33.

11. Pound, *Selected Prose*, p. 79.

12. Ibid., p. 77. For Pound's view of the Founding Fathers, see, among others, M. B. Quinn, *Ezra Pound: An Introduction to the Poetry* (New York: Columbia University Press, 1972), p. 128.

13. In the text of *The Cantos*, Chinese characters often appear beside their English translations, or sometimes alongside their English equivalents, as the quotation above illustrates.

14. Pound, *Selected Prose*, pp. 336–51.

15. In this discussion, I have followed James Legge's version of the chapter "The Works of Mencius" in Confucius, *Four Books*, pp. 610–20.

16. Van Wyck Brooks, "Introduction," in *Writers at Work: The Paris Review Interviews, Second Series* (New York: Viking Press, 1963), p. 58.

17. Ezra Pound, "Prolegomena," *Exile* 2 (Autumn 1927): 35.

18. T. S. Eliot, "Isolated Superiority," *Dial* 84 (1928): 47; Pound, "Date Line," in *Make It New*, p. 18.

19. Pound, *Letters*, p. xix.

20. Roy Harvey Pearce, *The Continuity of American Poetry* (Princeton: Princeton University Press, 1961), pp. 92, 88. See also Walter Sutton, "Introduction," in *Critical Essays*, p. 7. Sutton regards Pound as highly conscious of his role as an unacknowledged legislator for a Western society that he considers decadent, attempting single-handedly to create a culture and to order the chaos of his world.

21. Bacigalupo, *Trace*, pp. 5, 8.

22. Confucius, *Four Books*, p. 18.

23. Ezra Pound, "The Regional," *New Age* 25 (June 1919): 124.

24. Bacigalupo, *Trace*, pp. 56–57.

25. Pound, *Selected Prose*, p. 80. Elliot notes, in his "Poet of Many Voices" (in *Critical Essays*, p. 153) that it is hard to take Pound's proposed remedies for economic ills seriously, in themselves. Pound himself saw his own error of judgment when he wrote in 1972, in the Foreword to *Selected Prose*, "re USURY: / I was out of focus, taking a

symptom for a cause. / The cause is AVARICE." I am still not convinced that he has found the root of evil.

26. Bacigalupo, *Trace*, p. 53.

27. See, among others, Charles Norman, *Ezra Pound* (New York: Macmillan, 1960), pp. 359–61; and Noel Stock, *The Life of Ezra Pound* (New York: Random House, 1970), pp. 356, 361.

28. See Russell Hope Robbins, *The T. S. Eliot Myth* (New York: Schuman, 1951). Robbins accuses Eliot of lacking humanity and of anti-Semitism, among other things, and considers him not a man of letters but a propagandist. A different view is voiced by Peter Vierack, who sees pure poetry in the work of a man whose politics is impure ("Pure Poetry, Impure Politics, and Ezra Pound," in *A Case Book on Ezra Pound*, ed. William Van O'Connor and Edward Stone [New York: Crowell, 1959], pp. 92–103).

29. C. David Heymann, *Ezra Pound, the Last Rower: A Political Profile* (New York: Viking Press, 1976), p. 262.

30. M. L. Rosenthal, *A Primer of Ezra Pound* (New York: Macmillan, 1960), pp. 20–21.

Pound and the Troubadours (James J. Wilhelm)

1. See James J. Wilhelm, *The American Roots of Ezra Pound* (New York: Garland, 1985), p. 137.

2. All cantos quotations are taken from Ezra Pound, *The Cantos* (New York: New Directions, 1972). The citations are identified by canto number and page number, separated by a slash. In James J. Wilhelm, *The Cruelest Month* (New Haven: Yale University Press, 1965), the author traces in depth the tradition of using nature settings.

3. Ezra Pound, *Literary Essays*, ed. T. S. Eliot (New York: New Directions, 1954), pp. 94–108.

4. See Hugh Kenner, *The Pound Era* (Berkeley and Los Angeles: University of California Press, 1971), pp. 337, 340, and elsewhere.

5. Text in musical notes for *Chansons der Troubadours*, arr. Thomas Binkley, Das alte Werk SAWT 9567-B, 6.41126 AS.

6. Ibid.

7. See Ovid *Amores* 1.3.5, 2.17.1 and 5, 3.11a.12.

8. *Medieval Song: An Anthology of Hymns and Lyrics*, tr. and ed. James J. Wilhelm (New York: Dutton, 1971), pp. 151–52.

9. "Ab lo temps," lines 36–37. See *The Poetry of Cercamon and Jaufre Rudel*, ed. and tr. George Wolf and Roy Rosenstein (New York: Garland, 1983). This edition has *mirar* ("at first sight") instead of *entrar* ("it enters").

10. See Dante's *Inferno*, Canto 5.

11. See James J. Wilhelm, *Il Miglior Fabbro: The Cult of the Difficult in Daniel, Dante, and Pound* (Orono: University of Maine Press, 1982).

12. Ezra Pound, *The Translations of Ezra Pound* (New York: New Directions, 1953), p. 421.

13. *Ezra Pound: The Critical Heritage*, ed. Eric Homberger (London: Routledge, 1972), pp. 123–24; Ezra Pound, *Personae: Collected Poems of Ezra Pound* (1926; New York: New Directions, 1949), pp. 85–86, 100.

14. For a full translation, see *The Poetry of Arnaut Daniel*, ed. James J. Wilhelm (New York: Garland, 1981), pp. 2–5.

15. Pound, *Translations*, pp. 173–75.

16. Wilhelm, *Arnaut Daniel*, p. 51.

17. Pound, *Translations*, pp. 160–61.

18. Ibid., p. 157.

19. Ibid., p. 421.

20. Original text and translation from Wilhelm, *Arnaut Daniel*, pp. 42–43. Pound errs in translating *amas* as "loving"; see Pound, *Translations*, p. 423.

Where Memory Faileth (Michael North)

1. William Van O'Connor and Edward Stone, eds., *A Casebook on Ezra Pound* (New York: Crowell, 1959), p. 122; Ezra Pound, *"Ezra Pound Speaking": Radio Speeches of World War II*, ed. Leonard W. Doob (Westport, Conn.: Greenwood Press, 1978), p. 75; Ezra Pound, *Guide to Kulchur* (1938; reprint, New York: New Directions, 1970), p. 134.

2. Ezra Pound, *The Cantos* (New York: New Directions, 1972). References to this edition of *The Cantos* will give canto number and page number, separated by a slash. Pound, *Guide*, p. 187; Ezra Pound, *Selected Prose, 1909–1965*, ed. William Cookson (New York: New Direc-

tions, 1973), pp. 187 and 60; Ezra Pound, ABC of Reading (New York: New Directions, 1934), p. 92.

3. Ezra Pound, Literary Essays, ed. T. S. Eliot (New York: New Directions, 1968), p. 201; Pound, Ezra Pound Speaking, p. 58.

4. Pound, Selected Prose, p. 408; Pound, Guide, pp. 51, 53.

5. Pound, Guide, pp. 28, 33, 39.

6. Ibid., p. 45.

7. Pound, Essays, p. 299.

8. Blast 1 (1914): 46.

9. Pound, Guide, p. 134; Donald Davie, Ezra Pound: Poet as Sculptor (London: Routledge and Kegan Paul, 1965), p. 148.

10. David Eagleton, "Eliot and a Common Culture," in Eliot in Perspective, ed. Graham Martin (London: Macmillan, 1970), p. 287; Eliot, "Notes towards a Definition of Culture," New English Weekly, January 21, 1943, p. 117; Eagleton, "Common Culture," p. 288.

11. Pound, Selected Prose, p. 148.

12. Pound, Guide, p. 57.

13. Ibid., pp. 57, 60–61, 244.

14. Ibid., pp. 98, 194–95.

15. Michael André Bernstein, The Tale of the Tribe: Ezra Pound and the Modern Verse Epic (Princeton: Princeton University Press, 1980), p. 65.

16. See John J. Nolde, Blossoms from the East: The China Cantos of Ezra Pound (Orono: University of Maine Press, 1983), pp. 417–18.

17. Ibid., p. 418.

18. Ibid., pp. 99–100.

19. Bernstein, Tale of the Tribe, p. 55.

20. Peter Nicholls, Ezra Pound: Politics, Economics and Writing (London: Macmillan, 1984), p. 173.

21. Davie, Poet as Sculptor, p. 136; Pound, Ezra Pound Speaking, p. 246.

22. Pound, Guide, pp. 15, 32; Ezra Pound, Jefferson and/or Mussolini (New York: Liveright; London: S. Nott, 1935), p. v.

23. Ezra Pound, Selected Letters, 1907–1941, ed. D. D. Paige (1950; reprint, New York: New Directions, 1971), p. 127; Pound, Selected Prose, pp. 231, 163; Pound, Guide, p. 309.

24. Pound, Essays, p. 324; Pound, Letters, pp. 181–82.

25. Friedrich Nietzsche, The Use and Abuse of History, tr. Adrian Collins (Indianapolis: Bobbs-Merrill, 1957), p. 23. For an illuminating

discussion of Yeats' difficult relationship with his own memory, see James Olney, "W. B. Yeats's Daimonic Memory," *Sewanee Review* 85 (October–December 1977): 583–603.

Contributors

CHANG YAO-HSIN is chairman of the English department at Nankai University in Tianjin, China. He holds a Ph.D. from Temple University, where he wrote a dissertation examining Chinese influence on noteworthy American writers, including Emerson, Thoreau, and Ezra Pound. Dr. Chang is the author of *Greek and Roman Mythology* (Peking, 1981; reprint, 1984) and *English and American Literature: An Essay in Background and Historical Criticism* (Tianjin, 1986). He is senior editor of *Selected Readings in American Literature with Chinese Annotations* (Tianjin, 1986) and *An Anthology of American Literary Criticism with Chinese Annotations*. In addition, he is collaborating with his colleagues on *The History of American Literature*, a project in Chinese financed by the Ministry of Education of China. Dr. Chang is a member of the national standing committee of two scholarly associations in China: The Chinese Association for the Study of American Literature and the Chinese Association for the Teaching and Research of Foreign Literature.

LESLIE FIEDLER is Samuel Clemens Professor of English at the State University of New York at Buffalo. His numerous publications include *Love and Death in the American Novel*; *The Messengers Will Come No More*; and *Freak: Myths and Images of the Secret Self.*

ALFRED KAZIN is Distinguished Professor of Literature Emeritus in the Graduate School of the City University of New York. His numerous publications include *On Native Grounds: An Interpretation of Modern American Prose Literature*; *Bright Book of Life: Storytellers from Hemingway to Mailer*; and *An American Procession.*

HUGH KENNER is Andrew W. Mellon Professor of Humanities at the Johns Hopkins University. His numerous publications include books on Eliot, Joyce, Beckett, Wyndham Lewis, and Buckminster Fuller, as well as *The Poetry of Ezra Pound* and *The Pound Era.*

JAMES LAUGHLIN is the editor and publisher of New Directions Publishing Corporation, the publisher of Pound's poetry and prose. Pound's friend and student in 1934 at what he calls the Ezuversity, Laughlin himself has published both poems and prose, including *Selected Poems: 1935–1985*. His lectures and pieces on Pound will be published in 1987 by Gray Wolf Press. As Adjunct Professor of English at Brown University, he has taught seminars on the work of Pound and William Carlos Williams.

MICHAEL NORTH is Associate Professor of English at the University of California at Los Angeles. He is the author of *Henry Green and the Writing of His Generation* and *The Final Sculpture: Public Monuments and Modern Poets.*

MARCEL SMITH is Associate Professor of English at the University of Alabama. He has published poems, translations, and critical essays in a variety of journals.

WILLIAM A. ULMER is Associate Professor of English at the University of Alabama. His articles on nineteenth-century British poetry have appeared in *Victorian Poetry, Texas Studies in Literature and Language, The Keats-Shelley Journal, Studies in Romanticism,* and *JEGP.*

JAMES J. WILHELM is Distinguished Professor of Comparative Literature at Rutgers University. His numerous publications include *The Later Cantos of Ezra Pound; Dante and Pound; Il Miglior Fabbro: The Cult of the Difficult in Daniel, Dante, and Pound;* and *The American Roots of Ezra Pound.*

HARRIET ZINNES is Professor of English at Queen's College in New York. Poet, fiction writer, and art critic, she is the editor of *Ezra Pound and the Visual Arts,* a collection of Pound's writings about painting, sculpture, and architecture.

Index